OLIVER BURKEMAN

Oliver Burkeman is an award-winning feature
writer for the *Guardian*. He writes a popular
weekly column on psychology, 'This Column
Will Change Your Life', and has reported from
London, Washington and New York.

WITHDRAWN
FROM
STOCK

D1333689

ALSO BY OLIVER BURKEMAN

The Antidote:
Happiness for People Who Can't
Stand Positive Thinking

OLIVER BURKEMAN

HELP!

How to Become Slightly Happier
and Get a Bit More Done

VINTAGE

1 3 5 7 9 10 8 6 4 2

Vintage
20 Vauxhall Bridge Road,
London SW1V 2SA

Vintage is part of the Penguin Random House group of companies
whose addresses can be found at global.penguinrandomhouse.com

Penguin
Random House
UK

Copyright © Oliver Burkeman 2011
Copyright © Guardian News and Media Ltd 2010

Oliver Burkeman has asserted his right to be identified as
the author of this Work in accordance with the Copyright,
Designs and Patents Act 1988

First published by Vintage in 2018
First published by Canongate Books in 2011

penguin.co.uk/vintage

A CIP catalogue record for this book is available from the British Library

ISBN 9781784709655

Printed and bound in Great Britain by Clays Ltd, Elcograf S.p.A.

Penguin Random House is committed to a sustainable future
for our business, our readers and our planet. This book is made
from Forest Stewardship Council® certified paper.

MIX
Paper from
responsible sources
FSC
www.fsc.org   FSC® C018179

CONTENTS

INTRODUCTION

A few years ago, I started writing a weekly newspaper column in which I set out to solve the problem of human happiness. I was half-joking, of course. I was aware that the topic had already received an inordinate amount of attention from some of history's greatest thinkers – such as Aristotle, in his *Nichomachean Ethics*, and Paul McKenna, in his *Paul McKenna's Change Your Life in Seven Days: The World's Leading Hypnotist Shows You How* – and I didn't really imagine that I was going to make any staggering new breakthroughs. Besides, as a rational, non-gullible sort of person, I was allergic to the cheesy promises of self-help gurus. (Anthony Robbins, purveyor of $600-a-day motivational workshops, author of *Awaken the Giant Within*, and possessor of the most improbably chiselled jaw on the planet – I'm looking at you.) Even various not-so-cheesy explorations of happiness, by professional psychologists and philosophers, incurred my scepticism. This was perhaps because I'd grown up in the north of England, where people who go around looking too ostentatiously happy tend to be regarded as suspicious, and quite possibly American.

But I should be honest: if I was half-joking, I was also half-serious. Deep down, however much we cover it up with cynicism and wisecracks, isn't everybody at least half-serious about wanting to be happy? 'Happiness is the meaning and purpose of life, the whole aim and end of human existence,' observed one of the aforementioned great thinkers. (Hint: it wasn't Paul McKenna.) I mocked self-help gurus, and others who made a living dispensing tips and techniques for a more satisfying life, but I knew my mockery was at least partially defensive: it was much less embarrassing to dismiss all that stuff as mumbo-jumbo than to admit that I wanted some of what it promised. An awful lot of it *is* mumbo-jumbo, as I was to discover. But among those countless thousands of ideas for becoming happier, richer, more successful, more popular and more productive, surely there were a few that it might be useful to know about?

Fortunately, around the time I started delving into the topic, two developments were beginning to make happiness a slightly more acceptable subject for discussion among people who thought of themselves as sceptical and intelligent. The first was the explosion, among academic psychologists, of 'happiness studies', involving rigorous experiments designed to pinpoint the sources of human fulfilment. The other was the movement known as 'lifehacking', originating on the Internet, which disdained the grand promises of traditional self-help in favour of more modest goals: finding ways to beat procrastination, to keep your email inbox under control, and generally to simplify your life. Here, I felt much more at home, having always had a geeky fondness for time-management systems, to-do lists, personal organisers and the like. To put it another way, I was the kind of child who was liable to spend longer designing perfectly colour-coded exam revision timetables than actually revising for exams.

So I took a deep breath, tried to suppress my self-consciousness, and set out on an adventure through the world of popular psychology – a term I'm using loosely here to encompass self-help, happiness studies, lifehacking, and other ideas with an emphasis on practical implementation by a mass audience. I learned Neuro-Linguistic Programming from the experts, and listened to self-hypnosis CDs; I spoke to social psychologists, Buddhist psychotherapists and even a Scientologist, though to be honest he wasn't much help. I kept a gratitude journal; I tried to become a morning person; I tamed my out-of-control email; I attempted to stop complaining for 21 days. Above all, I read a vast number of books (including *Awaken the Giant Within* – I can't recommend it, I'm afraid) and research papers. I tried to approach it all in the spirit of a foreign correspondent, sending back reports from a strange new country, though I'm not sure I realised at the time exactly how strange some parts of it would be. This book is a record of what I found.

★

It's a little strange, when you stop to think about it, that the quest for happiness should have acquired such an embarrassing reputation, as if the desire to be a happier person were not the most universal of urges but rather a shameful predilection, like collecting Nazi memorabilia, or attending Michael Bolton concerts. This wasn't always the case. The ancient Greeks and Romans made no distinction between the noblest of all pursuits – philosophy – and self-help; for them, the whole point of figuring out what constituted 'the good life' was that you'd then be able to put your findings into practice. Why go to the trouble of asking the question, and formulating an answer, only to fail to follow your own advice? 'Philosophy's power to blunt the blows of circumstance is beyond belief,' was how Seneca the Stoic expressed this connection, and much of his work, viewed from a certain perspective, is really a collection of self-help tips. (If you're afflicted by the fear of failure, he advises at one point, try dressing in rags and subsisting on scraps of food for a week or two. That way, you'll always have the comfort of knowing you could tolerate it if you had to.)

This upfront, unashamed attitude towards seeking a better

life continued for centuries: even so esteemed a figure as Benjamin Franklin apparently felt little embarrassment telling the world about a notebook he carried, in which he listed 13 'virtues' – frugality, sincerity, that sort of thing – then made a habit of ticking off which ones he managed to exhibit on any given day. If you tried something similar in the twenty-first century, would you tell your friends about it? I'm not sure I would. Somewhere along the way, something changed.

Specifically, what happened was the Great Depression – and out of it, the modern incarnation of the movement known as Positive Thinking. The mid-1930s saw the publication of two books that bear much of the blame for the tacky, embarrassing, scam-filled era of self-help that followed: *How to Win Friends and Influence People* by Dale Carnegie, and *Think and Grow Rich* by Napoleon Hill. (The third main offender, Norman Vincent Peale's *The Power of Positive Thinking*, followed several years later.) It's not hard to see why they became bestsellers: in a world still reeling from economic devastation, their message to readers feeling pummelled by forces beyond their control was that they weren't as powerless as they had imagined. The security they'd once known might have vanished – but they could seize control of their own destinies simply by changing how they thought! 'Truly, thoughts are things,' writes Hill, and thus by cultivating 'persistence, and a BURNING DESIRE' – he has a troubling fondness for capital letters – whatever you can dream of can be yours. Seven decades later, the message persists: it is, for example, the philosophy behind Rhonda Byrne's mega-bestseller *The Secret*, which promises sports cars and expensive jewellery just by thinking really hard about them. I can't say this ever worked for me. But then again, perhaps my DESIRE wasn't BURNING brightly enough. Who knows?

The sad thing about all this is that positive thinking isn't actually all nonsense – and in any case it's far from the only possible approach to becoming happier, more successful, or more productive. Yet its numerous flaws have come to infect the whole field of popular psychology. Positive thinkers speak as if changing your life were rapid and easy (sometimes it is, but usually it isn't). They promise perfection, thereby setting you up for gloom and self-reproach when you fall short (which you will). Taken to extremes, the approach also leads to some exceedingly unpleasant conclusions: more than one writer has suggested that, since your thoughts create your reality, the victims of crime and poverty must be to blame for their suffering. Other times, the conclusions aren't sinister, just ridiculous – as in *Zero Limits*, a book by Dr Joe Vitale, in which the author relates the story of a doctor who 'cured a complete ward of criminally insane patients' without ever meeting them, merely by 'look[ing] within himself'. (Vitale's PhD, by the way, is from an institution in Arizona called the University of Metaphysics.) All of this also provides fertile ground for more straightforward con-artists and charlatans, preying on the desperate for financial gain. You can learn more about this in my ten-CD course, 'How to Spot a Self-Help Scammer', worth £1,999 but available for a short time only at the special price of £297.

The truth, though, as I now know, is that not all popular psychology is bad psychology. Yes, much of it will leave you unchanged, or even worse off than before – if only because your original problems will have been complemented by extra helpings of frustration and annoyance at failing to change. But some of it is deeply insightful, non-perfectionistic, practical, wise and humane. The trick is learning to tell the difference.

The other trick, of course, is putting it into practice – and the most obvious question to be answered about my encounters with self-help gurus, self-help books, happiness studies, motivational CDs, workshops and the rest is this: did it actually make me any happier, more productive, or more successful? I think it did. But not because I discovered some grand Principle of Happiness. Instead, I discovered numerous much smaller tips, techniques and insights, and it's these that make up the majority of what follows. I touch frequently on the big questions, but mainly as they relate to the smallest of matters: how to organise your to-do list, how to manage your day, how to handle awkward friends, how to get the most from holidays, how to become an early riser, how to organise your filing system.

If one big principle did emerge, it's that we probably ought to consider changing our ideas about change – about how we understand the whole notion of 'self-improvement'. Even if you hate that term, it's surely an accurate description of many of the activities that make up our lives. Yet to listen to the likes of Anthony Robbins – who advocates 'taking massive action' to go 'beyond the limits of the possible' – you'd think that the only way to achieve personal change was by going all-out, straining every sinew and revolutionising your life. This absolutist way of thinking is deeply seductive, even for those of us who don't share Robbins's hyperbolic demeanour: behind almost every New Year's resolution, for example, is the unspoken implication that whatever change we're trying to make – to start exercising more, eating better, procrastinating less – we're going to do it every day, perfectly, for the rest of our lives. I'd always wondered why my efforts at such extreme self-discipline seemed to fail every time. But then, gradually, I began to understand that real self-discipline is almost the exact opposite: the willingness to make small, incremental adjustments, to tolerate imperfection and bumpy progress, and not to throw in the towel in frustration the moment something starts to go wrong. In this sense, modest action (a phrase you won't find in Robbins's work) in fact takes more guts than massive action. But it has the inestimable advantage that it really works.

Then again, perhaps we also need to question what we mean by 'works', because achieving happiness, it soon became clear, doesn't necessarily mean feeling overjoyed all the time. Again, we have the positive-thinking movement to blame for the unhelpful idea that the goal of life – Aristotle's 'whole aim and end of human existence' – should be a state of unalloyed ecstasy. As the best scientific investigations into happiness make clear, there are two major problems with this. The first is that it simply isn't how we experience our most satisfying moments: when wrapped up in genuinely engaging work, or conversation, or interactions with our friends and families, it's more accurate to say that we're so absorbed that we're unaware of any kind of mood, overjoyed or otherwise. The second is that to experience a real sense of aliveness and fulfilment, the happiness researchers will tell you, you need to be exposed to a full symphony of emotions and not just the one-note melody of cheeriness. Too often, positive thinking is about closing off the possibility of negative emotions. But real happiness may also require a capacity for awe, curiosity and being comfortable with uncertainty – all characteristics that involve not closing off, but remaining open to the negative.

Something else I discovered: none of this needs to be complicated. The self-help industry thrives on complexity, for one obvious reason: it's much easier to charge money for books and workshops that are packed with details and intricate systems than those that aren't. It's true that self-help also thrives on the promise of quick fixes, but that's not the contradiction that it may at first appear to be: what's being promised is a quick solution provided that you follow complicated advice. The reality, it turns out, is that the best techniques and insights are simple, but not necessarily quick or easy. They're also not secret, which is an excellent reason to be wary of anyone promising to teach you the secret of happiness – or *The Secret* of happiness, for that matter. Not that I'm singling anyone out.

This is not, in any traditional sense, a book of advice. Indeed, my main advice is to be ceaselessly suspicious of the kind of people who set themselves up as sources of advice. But perhaps it can serve as a road map to the vast and sometimes bewildering territory of self-improvement, and also as a double-edged warning: to point out, on the one hand, that there's plenty of unhelpful balderdash out there – but that, on the other hand, even the best and most scientifically credible advice can appear off-puttingly schmaltzy. At some point, you're probably going to have to swallow your pride and try something even though some cringe-inducing guru recommends it.

As for the secret of human happiness – to be honest, I never quite did get around to solving it. But if I ever do, I'll have a *really* nicely organised filing system in which to store it.

1

CHANGE EVERYTHING, RIGHT NOW!

A Short Tour of Self-Help's Biggest Clichés

WHY YOU MIGHT NOT WANT TO
BOTHER FINDING YOUR PASSION

Few ideas have spread so rapaciously through the worlds of self-help and pop-spirituality as the notion of Finding Your Passion. Like a nasty outbreak of Dutch elm disease, it has infected entire populations, compelling publisher after publisher to use it in titles or subtitles. Motivational speakers, hypnotists and career coaches have also jumped on the passion wagon, taking a word hitherto reserved for those extra-special moments in life – making love, say, or being crucified – and applying it to the whole of it. Having found your passion, you're meant to Live Your Passion pretty much all the time. If this strikes you as exhausting, you're doing it wrong: you simply haven't found your passion yet.

It perhaps wouldn't be jaw-droppingly surprising if this manic focus on passion-finding were to have some counterproductive effects – and sure enough, Cal Newport, who runs the academic advice site Study Hacks, at calnewport.com, reports a chorus of cries for help from agonised students. They're worried they haven't found their passion; or they've found too many and can't decide between them; or their passion is working with animals, say, while their career path is electrical engineering. What all these worriers share, Newport notes, is a belief that passions are *a priori*, existing 'out there'; that, as he puts it, 'they're some mysterious Platonic form waiting for you to discover. This is a dangerous fiction.' Newport's main point is that passion is the feeling you get from mastering a skill, not some magical quality unrelated to hard work: you create passion, rather than 'finding' it, and for any given person there are probably

hundreds of activities that might suit. This has deeply practical
consequences. Suppose you dislike your job: if passions are
'out there', waiting to be found, you'll feel that quitting is
the only path to happiness, but if passions are made, it's
conceivable that doing the job differently might be an
alternative answer.

Beyond that, though, it's surely debatable whether a
(working) life governed by passion is necessarily that desirable
anyway. For me, at least, breathless excitement about a new
project is usually a sure sign that my interest is superficial
and will quickly fade. Far from feeling 'passionate' while
doing the things that mean the most, I swing between two
poles: on the one hand, grumpiness, because they're hard,
and hard things make me grumpy; on the other, no discernible
feelings at all, because I've slipped into the state of total
absorption that the psychologist Mihaly Csikszentmihalyi
calls 'flow'. And don't get me started on managers who seek
to 'cultivate passion' in employees. If 'finding one's passion'
means anything, it's surely an intrinsically personal process.
The act of presuming to help me with it, when you've
got a vested financial interest in the fruits of that effort, is
doomed from the start, no matter how well-meaning you
may be.

More generally, Newport suggests, demystifying passion 'is
liberating. It frees you from obsession over whether you are
doing the "right" thing with your life'. Almost any interest
'can be transformed into a passion with hard work, so there's
no reason to sweat choices such as [a university degree] or
your first post-college career'. If you're fortunate enough to
have the opportunity, just pick something that interests you,
he counsels. Then work hard at it. 'Passion' may not be worth
getting too excited about.

THE COMFORT ZONE CONUNDRUM

A good friend – a no-nonsense university scientist who's convinced that every self-help book, workshop or website in existence is weak-minded poppycock – recently took up skydiving. But perhaps we don't know each other as well as I thought, because he apparently believed I might say yes when he invited me to join him in jumping out of planes for no reason. It would be scary, he acknowledged, but then anything really worth doing is scary. Quite so. It doesn't follow, however, that everything scary is worth doing; running blindfold across a busy stretch of motorway would be terrifying, but personal growth would be unlikely. 'Do one thing every day that scares you,' Eleanor Roosevelt said, wisely, but she surely wasn't advocating a life spent sticking your fingers in electrical sockets.

This is also my problem with the idea of the Comfort Zone, a concept bandied about by self-help authors with alarming freedom. If you want to succeed at anything, they explain, try stepping outside your comfort zone, or preferably do something rather more muscular, such as (to quote the title of one motivational recording) *Smashing Out of the Comfort Zone* or even (to quote one blogger) 'Destroy[ing] That Comfort Zone To Bits'. The theory goes as follows: things that we owe it to ourselves to do – quit a job, demand a raise, ask someone out, end a relationship – will always seem horribly unpalatable, because they induce so much anxiety. What's rarely mentioned, however, is the obvious point that really stupid ideas are likely to seem unpalatable, too. If the idea of emigrating to Portugal fills you with resistance, is that because it's a great idea, or a terrible one?

Which isn't to say that the comfort-zone concept isn't useful, so far as it goes. Figuring out how to 'feel the fear and do it anyway', in the words of Susan Jeffers's classic and actually very level-headed bestseller, is surely a desirable skill. But the point isn't to force yourself to make frightening choices, or to 'seek the discomfort zone', as the exhaustingly frenetic management guru Tom Peters (or 'tompeters!', as he styles himself these days) recommends. Rather, it's a matter of ceasing to make the internal demand that you have to feel a certain way before you can take a particular action. The bookshelves heave with advice on how to feel confident in social settings, or motivated to take exercise, how to get inspired for creative projects, etcetera. But what if you just accepted that you felt afraid, or unmotivated, or uninspired, and went fearfully, unmotivatedly, uninspiredly onward?

'Give up on yourself,' wrote the late Japanese psychologist Shoma Morita, whose deadpan approach provides a refreshing respite from the legions of grinning positive thinkers. 'Begin taking action now, while being neurotic or imperfect or a procrastinator or unhealthy or lazy or any other label by which you inaccurately describe yourself. Go ahead and be the best imperfect person you can be, and get started on those things you want to accomplish before you die.'

JUST BE YOURSELF
(WHATEVER THAT MEANS)

'First and foremost, it's important to be yourself on a first date,' writes the relationship expert Lisa Steadman, author of *It's a Breakup, Not a Breakdown*, repeating romantic advice that well-meaning people have been offering since the neolithic period. It's not only dating, either: trawl the self-help shelves or magazine racks and you'll find that Just Being Yourself is the key to performing well at job interviews, making friends and winning at business negotiations. One book, *Authenticity: What*

Consumers Really Want, urges companies to just be themselves, too, and offers 288 pages of guidance, presumably because printing a book three words long would have been impractical.

What's unusual about Just Be Yourself isn't that it's questionable or infuriating advice, but that it's so meaningless, and in a curiously profound way. First, there's the problem of who you 'really' are. (Indeed, 'be yourself' is one translation of an old Zen *koan*, an instruction designed to blow the minds of trainee Buddhist monks because it can't be processed intellectually. The whole point of *koan*s is that they make no rational sense, which makes you wonder if recycling them as glib dating tips is wise.) Second, even if you know who you are, trying to act that way is impossible: as soon as you actively attempt to be genuine, you're being fake by definition. Nor can you leapfrog the paradox by deciding not to try; that's just another form of trying.

Most insidiously, the Just Be Yourselfers presume that 'who you are' is something fixed – an unchanging personality that potential friends, lovers and employers would instantly adore if you could only let it shine. It's true that some aspects of personality, according to psychological research, aren't very malleable.[1] But the work of the Stanford psychologist Carol Dweck strikes a killer blow to 'just being yourself'. The notion of personality as fixed, she demonstrates, is a big part of the reason we suffer from stress, anxiety and lack of success.[2]

Many of us, Dweck argues, carry around a 'fixed mindset': the implicit belief that our abilities are pre-set. That triggers anxiety, because we feel we must live up to our innate abilities. It lulls us into shirking effort because we think we're naturally good at certain things. And it causes us to avoid new challenges, in case they exceed our pre-set talents. By contrast, a 'growth mindset' – which can be learned – sees talents as developing, and early failures as feedback showing that progress is being made. You can Just Be Yourself, in a sense, but a 'yourself' that's inherently always changing. Dweck's studies show that merely learning about the fixed/growth distinction can transform people's stress levels and success. A growth mindset turns change into an adventure. It frees people from the burden of having to 'just' be themselves.

THE TROUBLE WITH MAKING FRESH STARTS

How to Disappear Completely and Never Be Found, published in 1996, contains instructions for committing what its author Doug Richmond calls 'pseudocide': faking your own death and starting again, unencumbered by the disappointments of the past. In some circles, pseudocide has become a punchline, thanks to the bungled efforts of John Darwin, aka 'Canoe Man', the Englishman who tried to fake his own death in a canoeing accident in 2002, then reappeared five years later, only to be arrested on suspicion of fraud, convicted and jailed. But Richmond's book makes the whole thing seem rather compelling. Even though my life is not, to the best of my knowledge, about to collapse in a pile-up of angry creditors, vengeful mistresses and arrest warrants, the idea of a pristine fresh start is enticing. Whose life is so perfect that they don't think they'd make a better job of it the second time around? Of course, I'm not desperate or foolish enough actually to do it. Pseudocides try to escape their existence. The rest of us buckle down and deal with things.

The awkward truth, though, is that a similar, if less extreme, addiction to 'fresh starts' underlies much of what we do. Self-improvement undertakings rest on the unspoken assumption that, by sheer force of will, we can cut ourselves free from unwanted personality traits once and for all. Unsurprisingly, self-help authors are the worst offenders: see, especially, books with titles such as *The Great Life Makeover* and *The Fresh Start*

Challenge. But fresh-startism seeps throughout private and public life: it is also, for example, the promise of most politicians campaigning for election, and of managers unveiling strategic plans to overhaul ailing companies.

One obvious problem with this is that people – and societies and companies – are hugely complex; any plan that singles out one aspect for total change ('From now on, no more procrastination!') is almost guaranteed to neglect other contributory factors. Then there's the 'focusing illusion': the way we chronically overestimate the effect that any one life change, such as moving or marriage, will have on our happiness. (In a famous study, sun-kissed Californians and residents of the often freezing American midwest both concluded that Californians must be happier because of the weather. In fact, there was little difference in their overall happiness levels.[3] Moving to sunnier climes may not be as transformative as you imagine.) We think we're making a fresh start when really we're adjusting only one or two of countless variables.

But there's a deeper problem: the concept of the fresh start suggests a very bizarre notion of the self. It implies that you can 'stand back' objectively from your personality characteristics, nominate some of them for change, then set to work. But, obviously, we *are* those characteristics; they define us. The self doing the work is the self being acted upon. This needn't mean change is impossible – clearly, it isn't – but it makes things vastly more complicated. It means we're inescapably implicated in what we're trying to leave behind, and it makes the idea of a truly fresh start highly suspect. *Start Where You Are* is the (very sensible) title of three different books on happiness, but the real point isn't that you *ought* to start where you are. It's that you have no option: you are where you are.

Cognitive therapists makes the valid point that it's not always useful to dissect the past: wallowing in childhood issues can be a poor route to contentment. But to try to escape entirely what makes you yourself is surely doomed by definition. It's like Baron Münchausen, lifting himself out of a swamp by his own hair. (He succeeded, but only in fiction.) Or like the pseudocidal efforts of Canoe Man. And look how that worked out for him.

THE ART OF ACCEPTANCE

Something I've had to learn to accept, as I wander the world of self-help, is an awful lot of people telling me to practise 'the art of acceptance'. Most books on self-improvement, of course, preach the opposite: they're about How to Transform Your Whole Life Completely. But a sizeable minority urges you to love your life, or your job, or the fact that you're single; they claim to tell you how to 'want what you have'. I've always bristled at this, mostly because it smacks of resignation – should you 'accept' being in an abusive relationship, or the destruction of the planet? (Other times, it seems like an excuse for self-indulgence: should you just 'accept' the fact that you drink too much, or treat others like dirt?) Maybe it's preferable to work in a sweatshop and not mind, rather than to work there in a boiling rage. But most of us wouldn't want to accept that fate at all. One book on acceptance, the bestselling 'business parable' *Who Moved My Cheese?*, urges employees to embrace the era of layoffs and longer hours. Accept your lot: it's such perfect management propaganda that some firms bought a copy for every worker.

It was the title of Tara Brach's book *Radical Acceptance* that made me think there might be something more to acceptance than this. Brach is no doormat: when she believed the United States was launching an illegitimate war against Iraq in 2003, she didn't complain at dinner parties; she protested at the White House, and was arrested and briefly jailed. 'Many people do use the notion of acceptance as passivity, and underneath that passivity there's an unwillingness to respond to life,' she told me. But real acceptance isn't about convincing yourself that something is good when it's bad. It's about fully acknowledging that what's happening is happening – 'accepting the realness of what's here' – which includes, crucially, your negative feelings about it. Accepting a situation 'doesn't mean you like it or say it's OK,' writes the psychologist Robert Leahy in *The Worry Cure*. 'It means you know it is what it is, and that is where you start from.'

That might sound like a cop-out. Most of us aren't delusional: we already accept that what's happening is happening. But, in fact, there's plenty of experimental evidence that we go to enormous lengths to avoid confronting, psychologically, what we dislike about our lives.[4] Our negative thoughts about our situation cause us emotional discomfort, so we try to stamp out the thoughts (positive thinking), or we just rail against them; we think we shouldn't be feeling bad. We try to deny how things are, and how we feel.

Looked at like this, accepting things doesn't mean putting up with them; indeed, it seems to be a precondition for real change. In one university study, for example, diabetics taught to acknowledge their negative feelings about their condition managed to stabilise their glucose levels.[5] 'The curious paradox,' as Carl Rogers famously put it, 'is that when I accept myself just as I am, then I can change.'

IS FOCUSING ON YOUR GOALS REALLY THE KEY TO SUCCESS?

One of the most stress-inducing books I've ever read is called *GOALS!*, by the business consultant Brian Tracy. It's not about soccer. It's about achieving your GOALS! in life – and those capital letters, along with the exclamation mark, may convey some sense of this book's strange capacity for tying my stomach into a knot, then tightening it. 'Living without clear goals is like living in a thick fog,' Tracy writes, forebodingly. His readers' sense of inadequacy thus stimulated, he's on hand with a solution: you need to define exactly what you want, then pursue it relentlessly. The only alternative is failure. 'Clear goals enable you to step on the accelerator of your own life and race ahead rapidly', he says, and the rest of the book purports to show you how. In fact, it reduces you – all right, me – to a gibbering, indecisive wreck, unable to define my GOALS! in the first place, and sulking resentfully about the shouty man who keeps telling me I've got to pursue them unceasingly, or else resign myself to becoming a person of no merit whatsoever.

You'll be familiar with Tracy's approach if you're unlucky enough to work in one of the many organisations where managers make themselves feel useful by requiring employees to define 'SMART' goals. 'Smart' stands for specific, measurable, attainable, realistic and time-bounded, and it's one of those acronyms that ought to make you suspicious from the outset, if only because it spells out a slightly too convenient word.

You may also have heard a story about the dangers of not setting goals, which is repeated in numerous self-help contexts. It usually goes like this. In 1953, students graduating from Yale University were asked if they had specific, written-down goals for their lives. Only 3 per cent said they had. Two decades later, the researchers tracked down the students, to see how things had turned out. And guess what? The 3 per cent who had formulated precise goals had accumulated more wealth than the rest put together.

This looks like an overwhelmingly powerful argument for setting goals – a scientific study to settle the matter, once and for all! – except for one problem: it never happened. (The magazine *Fast Company* was the first to debunk it publicly, basing its conclusions partly on an extensive search of Yale's archives from the 1950s.[6]) And so there's still little hard evidence that setting clear goals will make you richer, let alone happier.

Life, Brian Tracy is fond of saying, is like a buffet, not a table-service restaurant: you have to buckle down and work hard now, so that you can enjoy the fruits of your labour in the future. But this is surely exactly wrong – a recipe for storing up all your happiness for a brief few minutes on your deathbed, when you can look back smugly at your achievements. Contrast that with the insight of Stephen Shapiro, whose book *Goal-Free Living* makes the case that you can have some kind of direction to your life without obsessing about the specific destination. 'Opportunity knocks often, but sometimes softly,' he observes. 'While blindly pursuing our goals, we often miss unexpected and wonderful possibilities.' That sounds a lot more smart to me.

CONQUER YOUR PANIC ATTACKS NOW! QUICKLY! BEFORE SOMETHING REALLY BAD HAPPENS!

If you want to get really stressed out – unlikely, I realise, unless you're a method actor preparing for a role as a sleep-deprived heart surgeon being pursued by the mafia, or something – you could do worse than read *Change Your Life in 30 Days*, a bestselling book by the American TV life coach Rhonda Britten. 'By picking up this book you have committed to making dramatic changes in your life in the next 30 days,' she writes in the first paragraph. Hang on. I have?

It's unfair, though, to single out Britten, because her book is only one example of self-help schemes that promise massive transformations in highly specific periods of time. In fact, 30 days looks relaxed in comparison with *Change Almost Anything in 21 Days, Change Your Life in 7 Days, Shape Shifter: Transform Your Life in One Day* and, my favourite, *Transform Your Life in 90 Minutes*, an e-book that comes, bafflingly, with a 30-Day Fast-Start Guide for how to transform your life in 90 minutes.

As a sucker for quick fixes, it took me a long time to realise the problem. Deadlines induce stress and worry. They also lead to things getting done. But when the things you're trying to do include reducing stress and worry, the contradiction is obvious. Worse, these books exude perfectionism – the idea of total transformation, instead of just getting a bit better. 'I have been to sales seminars where the motivational speaker implied to 250 real-estate professionals from the same company that all of them could be the firm's number one salesperson next year,' Steve Salerno writes in *Sham*, an anti-self-help tirade that's overly negative, but spot-on in this instance. 'Consider . . . the psychic costs of coming up short in a philosophical system that disclaims the role of luck, timing or competition, and admits no obstacles that cannot be conquered by the sheer application of will.'

One day I may write a book called *Conquer Your Panic Attacks Now! No, Now! Quickly, Before Something Really Bad Happens!* Meanwhile, leading the field of authors who create more problems than they solve is the designer Karim Rashid, whose book *Design Your Self* is guaranteed to awaken obsessive-compulsive disorder in even laid-back readers. 'All your socks, t-shirts and underwear should be identical,' he advises. 'Impose order: line everything up perfectly.' Oh, and: 'All kitchen products should be hidden.' Why? So I can construct a hugely fragile existence that will send me off the scale with stress if someone gives me the wrong kind of socks?

'Perfectionism is the voice of the oppressor, the enemy of the people,' the infinitely more sensible essayist Anne Lamott observes in her book on writing, *Bird by Bird*. 'It will keep you cramped and insane your whole life . . . perfectionism is based on the obsessive belief that if you run carefully enough, hitting each stepping stone just right, you won't have to die. The truth is that you will die anyway and that a lot of people who aren't even looking at their feet are going to do a whole lot better than you, and have a lot more fun while they're doing it.' I'm not saying I'm any good at following this advice. But it is really, really good advice.

RANDOM ACTS OF KINDNESS

There appears to be some disagreement, though we can assume it's an extremely friendly disagreement, over who invented the concept of the 'random act of kindness'. Credit usually goes to the American peace activist Anne Herbert, who reportedly coined it – and its counterpart, the 'senseless act of beauty' – on a napkin in the early 1980s. Then again, a Californian college professor, Chuck Wall, claims to have thought it up in 1993; today, he tours as a motivational speaker and sells coffee mugs and fridge magnets extolling the virtues of spontaneous generosity. (Why not try asking him to send you some for free?) Every few years, the notion gets rediscovered as if it were new – by Oprah, in the movie *Pay It Forward*, or in Danny Wallace's book *Yes Man*; there are at least five other books on the topic. All of which baffles me slightly, since the only time I've been on the receiving end of an RAK – I was buying a sandwich in an airport when the woman ahead of me paid for it, vanishing before I could thank her – I wasn't suffused with a warm sense of humanity's interconnectedness. I was suffused with a feeling best expressed by an acronym that's popular online: WTF?

Maybe I'm atypically misanthropic. Or maybe not: the handful of studies conducted into people's responses to random generosity at least partly back me up. We know that bestowing kindness boosts the giver's mood. But recipients – according to a study in 2000 in which researchers handed gifts to members of the public – are frequently hostile.[7] 'If someone randomly does something kind for me, I'm on guard. I don't think that shows a fundamental cynicism or a deep distrust of mankind,' writes Gretchen Rubin, on her blog The Happiness Project, at happiness-project.com. 'It just shows that I think that most people act purposefully, and if I don't understand the purpose, I question their motives. It's not the *kindness* of the act that's the problem; it's the *randomness*.' This isn't to denigrate every good turn advocated by proponents of RAKs. But the really good ones aren't really random. Helping someone who's struggling with their shopping, say, is a targeted act. Random behaviour disorientates us.

Specifically, we wonder what the giver wants in return: reciprocity is so fundamental to human relationships that we assume something must be expected of us, too. Crafty salespeople can exploit this expectation: as the psychologist Robert Cialdini notes in his book *Influence*, we're so deeply primed to reciprocate generosity that customers who receive a free gift become far more likely to make a purchase 'in return'. (It works even when they dislike the seller. The reciprocity rule, Cialdini writes, 'possesses awesome strength, often producing a "yes" response to a request that, except for an existing feeling of indebtedness, would surely have been refused.') There's a reason the Hare Krishnas hand out flowers before soliciting donations: adopting that fundraising tactic transformed their finances.

Some despair of people like me, who are freaked out by the kindness of strangers: has trust in others really been so depleted? But there's something uncomfortably self-absorbed about an RAK that thrills the giver while confusing the receiver, and simultaneously triggering their inbuilt propensity to feel indebted. Here's to non-random, thought-through, rationally targeted kindness. A rubbish bumper-sticker slogan, lacking in anarchist pizzazz – but surely, on balance, a rather better thing.

INSTANTANEOUS PERSONAL MAGNETISM, AVAILABLE HERE!

Recently, I've been testing a series of self-improvement CDs called Paraliminals, which claim to use state-of-the-art methods to give you, among other things, 'instantaneous personal magnetism'. The problem with evaluating them, though, is that you can't really go around asking friends and colleagues whether they think you've been demonstrating instantaneous personal magnetism over the past few weeks.

Actually, that's not true. You can. I did. Uniformly, they gave me a slightly scared look, which made it clear that they agreed I was indeed demonstrating a new personality trait, no doubt about it. Just maybe not the one I'd intended.

Paraliminals' selling point is that they're not meant to be hypnotic, yet nor do you process them consciously. You can't: you're instructed to listen wearing headphones, and a syrupy-voiced American named Paul Scheele speaks two different scripts, one in each ear, at the same time. 'Your conscious mind finds it difficult to process two voices simultaneously, so it shuts down,' Scheele explains. (Afterwards, I made the following transcript of how his two scripts sound to the listener: 'Your image of yourself and there was a special delight notice your potential has always been on occasion that image of you leaking springs and weedy patches . . . ') At first, it made me feel car-sick. But then further thought did become impossible, which is definitely relaxing, whether or not it instils the promised benefits (as well as *Instantaneous Personal Magnetism*, there are CDs called *Ideal Weight*, *Anxiety-Free*, *Get Around to It* and *Positive Relationships*, each for around £19).

We're deep into the world of self-help 'technology' here, so Scheele doesn't even try to claim support from peer-reviewed studies. This kind of thing bothers some people immensely, but as long as hideous amounts of money aren't involved, I find it hard to worry. If I spend £19 on a CD called *Get Around to It*, then have a productive few days, as I did, why should I mind if it was really the placebo effect, or if I was subconsciously trying to get my money's worth? Even if I'm still waiting for the personal magnetism to kick in . . .

Paraliminals makes much of being cutting-edge, but none of this would have surprised the French pharmacist Émile Coué, born a century and a half ago. His 1922 book *Self Mastery through Conscious Autosuggestion* is best remembered for advising people to stand at the mirror, repeating: 'Every day, in every way, I'm getting better and better.' Today, that's a pathetic cliché: if you actually said it, you'd feel an instant failure. But that hardly means that what we tell ourselves – or buy CDs to tell us – is irrelevant.

Coué used the example of a plank, 30 feet long and one foot wide, placed on the ground: anyone could easily walk its length. 'But now . . . imagine this plank placed at the height of the towers of a cathedral. Who then will be capable of advancing even a few feet along this narrow path?' The only difference is that we imagine we can't. Coué concludes: 'We who are so proud of our will, who believe that we are free to act as we like, are in reality nothing but wretched puppets, of which our imagination holds all the strings.'

READ THIS BEFORE YOU DIE

When Dave Freeman, the co-author of *100 Things to Do Before You Die*, died in 2008 at the age of 47, having completed only half the items in his book, it was widely described as 'ironic'. This seemed harsh. Freeman's idea of a life well spent was one packed with exotic experiences (running with the bulls at Pamplona, a voodoo pilgrimage to Haiti), and he was busy living it; he never said the list was meaningful only if you got through the whole thing. No, let's be clear: 'ironic' is criticising before-you-die lists, as I'm about to do here, when your day job is being a journalist for *The Guardian*, which has published around 1,001 of them over the last few years. Still, here goes, because the phenomenon Freeman inspired is getting ridiculous.

In his wake came lists of albums to hear, movies to watch, artworks to see and then, subtly increasing the pressure, books of 1,001 foods you 'must' taste, buildings you 'must' visit. There are even parody gift books of things not to do before you die – a list that for me includes reading parody gift books. Oh, and there's *50 Places to Play Golf Before You Die*, presumably of boredom.

The obvious objection to all this is that fulfilment isn't about ticking off hedonistic thrills or compulsively seeking

novelty. 'The most radical thing you can do is stay home,' said
the poet Gary Snyder. Then again, there's now plenty of
evidence that actively pursuing unfamiliar experiences keeps
the brain limber, and makes time pass less fleetingly.[8] The
bigger problem is one that afflicts not just before-you-die lists,
but also the lists of tips that now dominate the self-help field
– 150 ways to de-stress your life, etcetera – which is that
reading lists of things to do is often a seductive way to avoid
doing them. It's spectatorhood: vicarious living, rather than
real life.

Tip-lists 'actively get in the way of fundamental improvement', observes Merlin Mann, who writes about creativity at
43folders.com, 'by obscuring the advice we need with the
advice that we enjoy. And the advice that's easy to take is so
rarely the advice that could really make a difference.'

It's surprising that the phrase 'before you die' gets tossed
around like this in a culture so intent on avoiding thinking
about death – or perhaps it's only because of that avoidance
that we can use it so casually. Actually thinking about a time
when we'll no longer be here is mindnumbing at best,
terrifying at worst. In *The Happiness Trap*, the psychologist
Russ Harris suggests a simple yet powerful perspective-shift
that's slightly less scary, though it scared me enough. Imagine
you're 80, then complete these sentences: 'I spent too much
time worrying about . . .' and 'I spent too little time doing
things such as . . .' (Apologies to octogenarian readers, who'll
have to modify this.) Of course, you might conclude that
voodoo pilgrimages are precisely your thing; Harris isn't trying
to be prescriptive. The difference is that your conclusion won't
be based on someone else's list. Dave Freeman spent his life
doing his thing. The trick is not to spend your life doing
Dave Freeman's thing.

2

HOW TO BE HAPPIER

Emotional Life

HOW TO STEP OFF THE
HAPPINESS TREADMILL

'Habit converts luxurious enjoyments into dull and daily necessities,' Aldous Huxley wrote, and I like to imagine the thought occurring to him as he sat at the wheel of his Lexus – the one with the in-car DVD player he was so excited about when he got it six months earlier. You want something because you think it'll make you happy, and maybe it does, briefly. But then the new thing loses its shine and you revert to your earlier, less happy state. This is the 'hedonic treadmill', and we all seem to be trapped on it. It doesn't just apply to material wealth, but that's where it's most obvious: in Britain, people are three times richer than they were in 1950, but barely any happier.[9] So when I heard that a psychology professor at the University of Miami might have discovered some methods for getting off the treadmill, I had to know more.

'The exciting idea here,' Mike McCullough told me, 'is that you might be able to recover some of the hedonic benefits from past events.' At cocktail parties, I suspect, atomic physicists look down their noses at McCullough when he tells them he's a gratitude researcher. But his experiments are rigorously scientific, and the results are startling. They show that people who keep regular 'gratitude journals' report fewer physical symptoms, more alertness, enthusiasm, determination, attentiveness and energy, more sleep, more exercise and more progress towards personal goals.[10] In a study by another researcher, college students were asked to make contact, just once, with someone towards whom they felt grateful. The positive effect on mood was huge at first, then tailed away, but only gradually: the difference, compared with a control group, was still detectible a month later.[11]

After spending some time immersing myself in this self-help business, I reached a fork-in-the-road moment: I realised I was going to have to choose between rejecting certain ideas because they sounded so corny, or accepting them because they work. Gratitude journals are at the extreme end of the cheesiness continuum, but the studies are hard to refute.[12] In stepping back and objectifying your circumstances in writing, you also step, however briefly, off the hedonic treadmill. You don't need to make it a regular habit, either. 'I don't keep a journal in any systematic way,' McCullough said, 'but I'll be in the car, or somewhere, and something I'm grateful for will come to mind, and then, yes, I will make sure that I really enjoy it.'

If you need another defence against the charge of corniness, consider this: the findings from gratitude research don't always imply that humans, deep down, are all that nice. Take the reported benefits of helping people in need, through volunteering or philanthropy. Isn't this just another way of throwing into relief the advantageousness of one's own situation, and thereby feeling gratitude for it?

I thanked McCullough, and told him I was grateful for his time. I meant it, actually, although afterwards it occurred to me that people probably say things like that to him every day, and think they're being funny.

THE HIDDEN PLEASURES OF WORRY

Is there a person on the planet who has ever been helped by being told not to worry? The slogan 'Don't worry, be happy' comes originally from the Indian mystic Meher Baba, but many of us know it best as a knuckle-gnawingly annoying 1988 song by Bobby McFerrin. And it's surely no accident that you only ever hear that song these days in war movies (*Jarhead*, *Welcome to Sarajevo*) where it's used as a savagely ironic counterpoint to the horrors on screen. When you stop to think about it, ordering anyone to stop feeling how they're feeling is an enormously thoughtless act, though we do it all the time – the phrase 'Cheer up!' being the most obvious example. The ultra-bestselling American pop psychologist Wayne Dyer calls worry a 'useless emotion', as if that should be enough for us to drop it. But his observation is itself useless. And, of course, wrong: there's a good reason why we've evolved to be able to map out, and plan for, how bad the future might be. It's just that sometimes it would be nice to be able to stop.

'I am an old man and have known a great many troubles, but most of them never happened,' Mark Twain is supposed to have said. Self-help authors, echoing Twain, like to claim that our brains can't distinguish between a real scenario and a vividly imagined one – so that, on a physical and emotional level, we respond to worries about a horrible event as if they were the horrible event. Some experimental evidence suggests this might be right: according to one recent study, it's possible to suffer the effects of post-traumatic stress disorder from events that were hallucinated.[13] One man in the study, delirious from liver disease, believed hospital staff were beating his son to death; he suffered the long-term psychological effects you'd expect if they actually had. It's not hard to extrapolate from this to what the smaller but real effects of our everyday fearful imaginings might be.

But with ordinary worry, unlike extraordinary trauma, there's something else to contend with – what the psychologist Edward Hallowell calls 'the hidden pleasures of worry'. 'One of the hidden pleasures is that worriers believe they're not safe unless they're worried – that the deal they make with fate is, if I torture myself by worrying, I won't be punished with bad outcomes,' he told me. 'The other hidden pleasure is that contentment is too bland; worry is more stimulating. We don't say, "She was gripped by contentment." The good news, though, is that worriers tend to be the smartest, most creative people we've got. It takes a lot of imagination to dream up all these worries.'

Hallowell's number one prescription is 'never worry alone'. I asked why, half-expecting some complex neurological explanation. 'It's just a fact of human nature. We're better in connection than in isolation.' This works with worry, as with any area of life. 'If you're in a big room alone in the dark, you feel frightened,' Hallowell said. 'If you're with someone else, you laugh.'

WHY IT REALLY IS BETTER TO GIVE THAN TO RECEIVE

The other day, I learned of some breakthrough psychological research which proves that contributing to good causes stimulates the same parts of the brain as receiving large sums of money – only more so.[14] Giving to others, it turns out, really may be the key to happiness. About 35 minutes later, I ran into a 'charity mugger', collecting for a human rights organisation, and became consumed with a quasi-homicidal rage that only worsened as he trotted after me down the street, stoking fantasies of breaking his clipboard in two and dropping it in pieces at his feet. There seems to be a contradiction here. Some possible conclusions: a) my brain is hardwired wrongly; b) the psychology researchers screwed up; or c) there are only certain conditions under which giving makes you happy, and being bullied by an out-of-work actor with a goatee isn't one of them.

The researchers, at America's National Institute of Neurological Disorders and Stroke, scanned people's brains while they played a computer game that gave them opportunities to win cash prizes or make donations to charity, sometimes at a cost to their own pocket, sometimes not. All these procedures lit up regions of the brain associated with the release of the 'pleasure chemical' dopamine – but giving large sums at a cost to oneself did so the most. (It also triggered the production of oxytocin, the 'cuddle hormone', which is associated with forming strong attachments.) Nor was any of this down to the givers thinking they'd get a pat on the back for being so selfless: their donations were anonymous.

Richard Dawkins has argued convincingly why this happens: what looks like altruism, he says, is a hangover from an era when we lived in communities so tiny that anyone we ran into would most likely be genetically related, or, alternatively, in a position to harm our survival if they weren't on our side. (To witness Dawkins's own hyper-evolved capacity for withering put-downs, watch one of the online videos in which he tries to convince creationist college students of this argument.[15])

But that only hints at why it feels good to do things that benefit our genetic legacy. It doesn't address the moral quandary. Can it be right to choose who I give to on the basis of how it makes me feel? It's possible, in theory, that giving hundreds of pounds to my goateed haranguer would have been the most efficient way to get money to the people who needed it most, even though I'd have ended the transaction feeling annoyed. Contrastingly, giving to people sleeping rough triggers a warm inner glow – but numerous homelessness organisations advise against it. Then again, it would be nonsensical to give only when it made me feel bad to do so, wouldn't it?

Such are the mental acrobatics, it seems, in trying to make selflessness selfishly rewarding. At least the US researchers were clear on the bigger point: giving makes you happier than getting. So, as a purely philanthropic gesture, I'm willing to receive your cheques care of this book's publisher.

YOU REGRET WHAT YOU DON'T DO, NOT WHAT YOU DO

If you were organising a dinner party in nineteenth-century Copenhagen, and wanted to be sure of having someone in the mix who'd keep the conversation upbeat, you probably wouldn't have invited Søren Kierkegaard. 'Marry, and you will regret it; do not marry, and you will also regret it,' wrote the Danish theologian, philosopher and notorious grumbler. In life, he observed, there are always 'two possible situations: one can either do this or that. My honest opinion and my friendly advice is this: do it or do not do it. You will regret both'. And you'd certainly regret having invited Kierkegaard round for dinner: what a buzz-kill.

But he had a point – not so much about regret as the anticipation of it. We approach decisions, big or small, burdened by the fear that whatever choice we make, we'll come to regret it. Sometimes this paralyses us; other times it makes us do irrational things. People who buy lottery tickets know the chance of winning is infinitesimal, but a recent study by researchers at Northumbria University shows that many keep playing out of anticipatory regret.[16] If you use a regular set of numbers, it's intolerable to imagine how you'd feel if you missed a week and those numbers came up.

Worse, we seem predisposed to anticipate regret wrongly. Faced with some fear-inducing opportunity (should you leave your job? ask that person out?), we habitually believe we'll regret acting more than not acting, when the opposite is true.

A classic approach in decision theory, a branch of economics, asks people to predict the regret felt by two investors: one who misses out on a large sum because he fails to switch his shares from company A to company B, and another who misses out on the same amount because she moves her shares away from company B to company A. Most people assume the switcher, the proactive one, will feel worse, and in certain experimental settings, with one-off decisions about hypothetical companies, that's sometimes true. But in his book *If Only*, the psychologist Neal Roese argues that when it comes to real-life choices, 'if you decide to do something and it turns out badly, it probably won't still be haunting you a decade down the road. You'll reframe the failure, explain it away, move on, and forget it. Not so with failures to act'.[17] You'll regret them for longer, too, because they're 'imaginatively boundless': you can lose yourself for ever in the infinite possibilities of what might have been. In other words: you know that thing you've been wondering about doing? Do it.

And don't worry about burning bridges, because Roese's other counterintuitive conclusion is that irreversible decisions are regretted far less. This may be why education and career figure at the top of the list of the areas in which people (or Americans, to be precise, according to a 2005 study) harbour regret: it's fairly easy to go back to university or change jobs. Family and finances come a little lower: it's harder to decide, late in life, to have (or un-have) children, or to become a millionaire.[18] But if you do have regrets, Roese says, don't try to eradicate them: mild regrets serve 'a necessary psychological purpose', crystallising the wisdom we need to make more enriching future choices. Never regretting anything – with apologies to Edith Piaf and Robbie Williams – may ultimately be a sign of shallowness.

THE FUNNY THING ABOUT LAUGHTER

A few years ago, Robert Provine, who is probably the world's leading laughter scientist, set out to discover what cracks us up. He and his researchers monitored thousands of human interactions, noting who said what, and who laughed in response. Strap on your surgical ribcage support right now, because I'm about to reveal some of the most hilarity-inducing lines: 'I know.' 'I'll see you guys later.' 'I see your point.' 'It was nice meeting you.'[19] (Dry your eyes, take a few deep breaths, and we'll continue.) 'Most pre-laughing dialogue,' Provine later wrote in his book *Laughter: A Scientific Investigation*, 'is like that of an interminable television situation comedy, scripted by an extremely ungifted writer.'

This is great news for extremely ungifted sitcom writers, but a little mystifying for everyone else. Most of us, presumably, want to laugh more than we do; after all, we spend about a third as much time laughing as people did in the 1930s, according to one 'laughter therapist', Carole Fawcett, and it's commonly held – albeit without much scientific backing – that as adults we laugh vastly less than we did as children. Yet seeking out humorous people, books or TV shows wouldn't seem to be the answer: laughter and humour, Provine's research indicated, aren't very closely related.

'Laughter existed before humour,' Provine told me, shortly before doing an impression of a chimpanzee laughing, the brilliance of which I sadly can't convey in print. 'It's the ritualised sound of rough-and-tumble play.' The sound primates have always made, in other words, when they're socialising energetically. It's not a response to something funny, but an instinctive bonding mechanism. Or as Provine puts it: 'The key ingredient to laughter is another person, not a joke.'

Nowhere is this clearer than in sexual politics. Provine analysed thousands of personal ads and found that women disproportionately sought men with a good sense of humour, while men disproportionately claimed to possess one. In fact, he reckons, nobody was really talking about humour: the women wanted men who made them laugh, and the men wanted women who would laugh when they spoke. This suggests one way to diagnose the health of any given heterosexual relationship: notice how frequently the female partner laughs.

Looking at things this way also casts doubt on the notion of laughter as medicine – the 'laugh your way to wellness' approach pioneered by the radical American doctor Patch Adams. Perhaps the real reason that people who laugh more sometimes seem to be healthier, or to recover more rapidly from illness, is simply because they spend time with others.

'If you want to laugh more, place yourself in situations where laughter's more common,' Provine said. 'Not a comedy club, but simply spending more time with your friends.' And can laughter make you well? He sighed. In fact, Provine argues – controversially – that there's a slight negative correlation between a happy outlook on life and longevity, perhaps because optimism encourages risky behaviour. 'I don't want to come off as a total curmudgeon . . . but laughter makes us feel good. Our lives will be better if there's more of it. Isn't that enough?'

WRITE YOURSELF BETTER

In an interview looking back on his time in power, Tony Blair once said he regretted that he'd never had the discipline to keep a diary. He was talking, one assumes, about the kind of brief daily journal that he could later have published, politician-style, in a heavily edited and legacy-burnishing form, or used as the basis for his memoirs. This is as opposed to the kind of diary celebrated in such self-help books as *Journaling from the Heart, Embrace Your Life through Creative Journaling* and *Inner Journeying through Art-Journaling* – or in the magazine *Personal Journaling*, which is, intolerably, a journal about journaling. It's hard to imagine many politicians keeping this kind of diary, which calls for introspection and self-questioning. At the risk of blinding you with my unrivalled access to the inner circle of British politics, you can take it from me that No. 10 Downing Street has never subscribed to *Personal Journaling* magazine.

And rightly so, perhaps: you surely don't have to be some stiff-upper-lipped British throwback from another era to find the cult of journaling a bit wallowingly self-absorbed. Nonetheless, I was surprised to find agreement on this point from Professor Jamie Pennebaker, the world's leading scientific authority on the emotional benefits of writing things down. 'Oh, yes, you can definitely wallow,' said Pennebaker, an experimental psychologist at the University of Texas. 'I've noticed how people who journal a lot can seem to tell the same story, over and over again.'

What's startling, though, are the proven mood-enhancing powers of writing when it's done in a more focused way. Pennebaker's research shows that when people who've experienced trauma are asked to write about it – for 15 minutes a day for four days, no more – they show rapid improvements in wellbeing compared with those who write about something else.[20] In one extraordinary experiment, by John Weinman at King's College, London, tiny, identical skin wounds were inflicted on patients, some of whom were then asked to spend a few minutes, for a few days, writing about stressful events they'd experienced. The wounds were monitored with ultrasound, and the skin damage healed faster among those who wrote about their feelings.[21]

Strange things happen when people write in this way. Over several days, their language shifts from being emotional to being more thoughtful; from being dominated by 'I' and 'me' to 'we' and 'us'. So it seems writing works not only as catharsis but in a practical way, too, helping us objectify problems, step out of self-absorption, and look to solutions. It isn't a case of 'a problem shared is a problem halved', either: nobody else need ever see what you write for the technique to have an effect.

'Years ago, my wife and I went through a difficult patch in our marriage,' Pennebaker recalled. 'We were in the midst of all sorts of ugly tension, and I just sat down and started writing. Even within the first day, it was all starting to come together. I threw away what I wrote, because I didn't want my wife to see it.' They're still married.

DOES HAVING CHILDREN REALLY MAKE YOU HAPPIER?

When you don't have children – as I don't, thus far – one entertaining thing to do with friends who do is as follows. Wait until they're gazing, lovestruck, into the eyes of their newborn baby, tucking their toddler into bed, or proudly watching their 21-year-old graduate. Then creep up behind them, slap down a copy of the *Journal of Marriage and Family*, volume 65, number 3, and triumphantly declare: 'Ha! You may think parenthood has changed your life for the better, but, in fact, the statistical analyses contained herein, along with numerous other studies, demonstrate conclusively that having children makes people, on average, slightly less happy than before!'[22] Then walk away cackling. They may never speak to you again, but that won't matter: you will have won the argument, using Science.

Here's the thing, though: the studies really do suggest that 'having children does not bring joy to our lives', as Nattavudh Powdthavee, of York University, put it in an overview of the research published in *The Psychologist*.[23] For most people, parenthood leads to no increase, or even a decline, in satisfaction – a finding so counterintuitive that a common response is to assume the studies must be flawed. But there's little mileage in attacking the methodology, which often involves asking thousands of people, repeatedly over years, to rate their overall satisfaction with life. Some may be bad at recalling how happy they've been recently; some may lie. But there's no particular reason to think that would skew the results against parenthood. If anything, the taboo against admitting to regretting having kids may push things the other way.

What makes us so certain that parenthood will make us happy, Powdthavee argues, is the notorious 'focusing illusion': contemplating any major alteration in our circumstances, we overrate the effect it will have. We imagine living idyllically after making millions; in fact, sudden wealth leaves most people largely emotionally unchanged.[24] Besides, the belief that children make us happy is what the psychologist Daniel Gilbert calls a 'super-replicator': civilisation depends on it, and those who disagree tend not to have kids, so their views don't percolate down the generations.

More intriguing to me, though, is how many parents insist parenthood is fulfilling. Assuming they're telling the truth, and assuming the life-satisfaction studies mentioned above aren't bunkum, this raises mind-bending possibilities. Are fulfilment and satisfaction fundamentally different? We know fulfilment is different from pleasure, obviously: most things worth doing

– child-rearing included – aren't 24-hour fun. But the researchers weren't asking about fun; they were asking about life satisfaction. Suppose you're a parent whose survey responses showed you were less satisfied than when you weren't a parent. Now suppose someone else asks you if parenthood is fulfilling, and you glow with conviction as you answer yes. Which response is the more 'true'? I'm baffled. I have no idea. And I fear there's only one way to find out.

ARE YOU PAYING ATTENTION?

Too often, our lives pass us by. In what is possibly my all-time favourite Ridiculous Psychological Experiment – and, believe me, that's saying something – a researcher stopped people on a university campus and asked for directions. Halfway through the exchange, two accomplices, posing as workmen, barged between them, carrying a door. By the time they had gone, the researcher had been replaced by someone different. According to post-experiment interviews, a majority never noticed.[25]

This pervasive sense of being distracted feels like a modern affliction – a function of too much email, too many mobile phones, or the result of having relentlessly bad television as the backdrop to our lives. So it's reassuring to find that it was a problem in 1910, too, when Arnold Bennett wrote *How to Live on 24 Hours a Day*, one of the most eccentric yet timelessly wise books of advice you're ever likely to read.

Bennett's audience was the new class of suburb-dwelling commuters: gents who travelled into town for white-collar jobs that held out the promise, for the first time since the industrial revolution, that work could be fulfilling. But it wasn't. Instead, it led to 'the feeling that the years slip by, and slip by'.

Bennett is a stoic. You don't have to love your job, he says, but if you don't, don't let it define your life. The 'typical man . . . persists in looking upon those hours from ten to six as "the day",' and the rest as useless 'margin'. 'You emerge from your office. During the journey home you have been gradually working up the tired feeling. The tired feeling hangs heavy over the mighty suburbs . . . like a virtuous and melancholy cloud.'

Responsibilities outside work don't register much for Bennett – parental duties go unmentioned; housekeeping and cookery are done by servants. But his central idea echoes down the decades: cultivate your capacity to pay attention – to not let life go by in a distracted blur – and time expands. His book is full of techniques for finding a few hours a week to study music, history, public-transport systems. His point isn't what you pay attention to; it's that you pay attention. 'The mental faculties . . . do not tire like an arm or a leg. All they want is change – not rest, except in sleep.'

It's easy to misinterpret advice like this as the barking of a drill sergeant who wants you to cram more achievements into your day. But Bennett's insight is that zoning out is tiring, not relaxing; half-hearted semi-focusing causes life to feel like an exhausting blur. He was born in 1867, and died in 1931, so he never had to confront reality TV-watching, or mindless web-surfing – the things we do (or half-do) today to relax, but that leave us curiously drained. One suspects he wouldn't have been a fan.

THE WILDERNESS REMEDY

'I went to the woods because I wished to live deliberately,' wrote the nineteenth-century philosopher Henry David

Thoreau, describing his two-year exile to Walden Pond, in Massachusetts. He wanted, he said, 'to front only the essential facts of life, and see if I could not learn what it had to teach'. It slightly spoils Thoreau's lovely book, *Walden*, when you visit the pond and find it's just a short hike from the nearest town, or when you learn – though he never mentions it – that he had someone to do his laundry. And all on a private income: bloody trustafarians. Yet his point stands: there's something fundamental, something transformative, about spending time in wild nature.

This may seem so obvious that there's no reason to say anything more about it, and self-help authors rarely do: when you've got several hundred pages to fill, innovative methods for achieving happiness are more appealing than a simple instruction to put down the book and hit the road in search of somewhere where the sky is bigger. But the question of why nature makes us feel better turns out to have puzzled psychologists for years.

'The wilderness inspires feelings of awe . . . one's intimate contact with this environment leads to thoughts about spiritual meanings and eternal processes,' ventures one philosophical investigation of 'wilderness effects'.[26] Polls over the years have shown that 82 per cent of us have 'experienced the beauty of nature in a deeply moving way'; 45 per cent report an 'intense spiritual experience' in such settings.[27] These are surprising numbers, given that we're generally held, ever since the industrial revolution, to be rushed off our feet and out of touch with our emotions. Wilderness experiences seem to slice through all that. I can tell you, for example, about an encounter with a herd of deer, on Skye, on a late-autumn afternoon not long ago, and you'll know how I felt even if you've never been near the place.

But why? One part of the reason for this near-universal

response seems to be about control. We spend our lives swinging back and forth between believing we have more control over the world than we do, and feeling, just as wrongly, that we have none. The former delusion is the root of much stress: why would you bother feeling stressed if you truly knew how little you controlled your future, or others' behaviour? The latter is linked to depression, as the researcher Martin Seligman has demonstrated: he calls it 'learned helplessness'.[28]

Nature seems to reset this wild pendulum, restoring realistic balance. On one hand, elemental landscapes drive home how tiny we are, and how powerless. On the other, any encounter with nature, even a two-mile stroll, requires self-reliance and demands that you take responsibility for what you can control: you have to not get lost, not fall off cliffs. Even a pot plant on your desk – a wilderness in miniature – requires careful tending (which you can control) but might die (which you can't control). Psychologists refer to this realistic sense of our own powers, combined with some other useful qualities, as 'hardiness'. That seems a worthwhile state to aspire to – and if the prescription is spending more time amid mountains, moors and oceans, who would decline the treatment?

ON SWEATING THE SMALL STUFF

Among the most obvious portents of the impending collapse of western civilisation is the fact that you can now buy something called *Chicken Soup for the Chocolate Lover's Soul*, which is available as a gift box containing a book – part of the dispiritingly unstoppable *Chicken Soup for the Soul* series – and a bar of chocolate. There's also *Chicken Soup for the Wine Lover's Soul*, which comes with a corkscrew, and *Chicken Soup for the Tea Lover's Soul*, which features, confusingly, tea-flavoured chocolate. Apparently, the temptation to take a successful brand and spin it into ever more absurd cash-generating niches was irresistible. The logical conclusion is surely *Chicken Soup for the Chicken Soup Lover's Soul*, which will come with some chicken soup; at this point, earthquakes will consume London and New York, and God will burst into tears.

So it's to the credit of Richard Carlson, who died in 2006 aged 45, that after writing *Don't Sweat the Small Stuff . . . And It's All Small Stuff*, he published around 20 spin-offs (*Don't Sweat the Small Stuff at Work*, and suchlike) without once entering the realm of self-parody. Like *Chicken Soup*, the *Don't Sweat* books sold prodigiously. Unlike them, however, they're full of calm good sense, anchored in Carlson's understanding that stress obeys an ironic principle: when really big crises occur, people often find inner strength; it's the little things that drive us crazy. Deep down, we know we can't escape bereavement, and maybe illness or divorce, but we think we shouldn't have to deal with queues or irritating colleagues.

Carlson's suggestions aren't complex. They include 'make peace with imperfection', 'nurture a plant', 'choose being kind over being right' and 'allow yourself to be bored . . . [if you] don't fight it, the feelings of boredom will be replaced by feelings of peace'. He doesn't claim his insights are new. But that modesty is central to his message: we don't need new information on how to be happy anywhere near as much as we need a dose of perspective.

Advice on how to get more done, feel better, find a soulmate, etcetera, can be useful, but it subtly reinforces the notion that achieving such goals is overwhelmingly important, which fuels stress. Sometimes it's more helpful to be jolted into remembering that we'd be OK without those things, and that most things we worry about seem absurd a few weeks later.

There's a sort of serenity, too, in realising that even the greatest calamities won't mean much in 100 years. That jolt can come from a good self-help book, which puts you in the author's shoes, and gets you out of your head. But it also can come from travel, or writing down problems: anything that puts you in a third-person relationship to yourself. It isn't really 'all small stuff', as Carlson acknowledged, but there's always a perspective from which even the biggest stuff is, in some sense, handleable. The challenge is to keep making that shift in vantage point, rather than staying locked in position, forever seeking sources of comfort to deaden the negative feelings, marinating in Chicken Soup.

ANGER MANAGEMENT

On the subject of anger, I have a self-serving theory, which is that my quickness to become furious about petty matters – chiefly, the price of train tickets and the strange way that any street I move to instantly becomes the site of major construction works – is actually a good thing. After all, doesn't it show that I'm fortunate enough not to harbour far deeper, more destructive rages against my parents, or bullies from childhood, or society in general? I realise there's an alternative interpretation, which is that I'm just an irritable curmudgeon. But that isn't half so consoling whenever I find my fists involuntarily clenching as I hear some train company representative tell me I could have paid a reasonable price for my ticket if only I'd booked it two years in advance.

What one should do on such occasions, self-help authors have always claimed, is find a harmless way to vent. 'Punch a pillow – or a punching-bag,' writes John Lee in his book on anger, *Facing the Fire*. 'Punch with all the frenzy you can. If you are angry at a particular person, imagine his or her face on the pillow or punching-bag ...You will be doing violence to a pillow or punching-bag so that you can stop doing violence to yourself by holding in poisonous anger and hatred.' This is the 'catharsis hypothesis' – the idea that it's better out than in – and in the world of pop psychology it has the status of an article of faith. It gets applied to worry, too, which explains 'a problem shared is a problem halved'. But the real problem, it turns out, is with the hypothesis itself. (Also: who actually owns a punching-bag?)

We're so accustomed to thinking of our emotions using the metaphor of a pressure-cooker, or a bottle with a cork in it, that we're barely aware we're doing it. According to this 'hydraulic metaphor', emotion 'builds up inside an individual, similar to hydraulic pressure in a closed environment', the anger researcher Brad Bushman says, paraphrasing the received wisdom that his work sets out to challenge. 'If people do not let their anger out, but try to keep it bottled up inside, it will eventually cause them to explode in an aggressive rage.'

But Bushman's experiments indicate that venting actually makes things worse.[29] So do some others. In one classic study, participants were insulted, then some were asked to hammer nails into wood for several minutes. Subsequently, given the chance to criticise the person who'd insulted them, the nail-pounders were significantly more hostile.[30] Maybe the hammering provided some physiological relief, but their underlying anger had been stoked. Rather than punch a pillow, Bushman recommends doing something incompatible with anger, such as reading or listening to music. That won't address the cause of the anger, but it will leave you in a better frame of mind to do so.

Likewise, a recent study focusing on teenage girls concluded that the obsessive discussion of worries – 'co-rumination' –

often exacerbated negative emotions: a problem shared isn't always a problem halved.[31] This isn't an argument for bottling things up: talking, obviously, is a crucial way of finding solutions to problems. But it may be an argument for realising that we're much more complex than bottles.

SMILE! (IT HELPS PREVENT BANK ROBBERIES)

If you try to rob a bank in Seattle in the near future – I'm not suggesting you test this out; just take it on trust – you could be in for a surprise. Bank robbers, of course, do everything they can to try to avoid surprises. ('What I love about this job is its unpredictability – you never know what's going to happen!' is one of the things you never hear bank robbers say.) But the surprises they are worried about are things like the sudden appearance of police officers, or quick-witted customers trying to tackle them to the ground. The really surprising thing about the FBI's innovative Safecatch system, in operation in Seattle, is that it involves training bank employees to terrify robbers by smiling at them.

'If you're a legitimate customer, you think, "This is the friendliest person I've met in my life." If you're a bad guy, it scares the lights out of you,' one bank executive told the Associated Press. Bank robberies almost halved, year-on-year, after the scheme became widespread. Smiling pierces the anonymity thieves cultivate, creating precisely the connection they're desperate to avoid. You didn't think the grinning 'greeters' in the doorways of big American shops (and, increasingly, British ones) were really there to make you feel welcome, did you?

Of course, a smile produced in the high-stress context of a bank robbery is going to be a fake one. But that doesn't necessarily spoil the effect. As part of his research into the bodily signs of lying and deception, the psychologist Richard Wiseman revealed how bad we are at telling real smiles, which involve the eye muscles, from fake ones, which use only the mouth.[32] There's something else researchers keep confirming, though – an utterly strange phenomenon which accords with none of our beliefs about how emotions operate: fake smiling even works on ourselves.

In one landmark study, German students were called into a lab and told they would be helping to test different ways for paraplegic people to hold pens. Some were asked to hold a pen between their teeth – an action that produces an involuntary smile. Others were asked to hold it with their lips, which induces a frown. Soon after, they were shown a cartoon and asked to rate how funny they found it. The teeth-holders were unequivocally more amused.[33]

You can, of course, experience this effect for yourself. Take a few deep breaths and notice your mood. Then pull your lips into an exaggerated smile and hold it for three or four seconds. You should notice an elevation in your mood. Alternatively, perhaps you notice that the person sitting beside you on the bus is starting to look unsettled, and wondering again why it's always them who ends up next to the weird, grinning passenger.

This is the problem with psychology experiments: do them in universities and people give you research funding; do them on public transport and all they give you is funny looks.

THE INVENTION OF STRESS

Stress was invented in 1936, when the Hungarian biologist Hans Selye defined it as 'the non-specific response of the body to any demand for change'. So while it would be unfair to blame Selye for the fact that modern life is so stressful, he does deserve some blame for the epidemic of articles about the 'stress epidemic' – have you noticed how reading them stresses you out? – and for books such as *Stress-Free in 30 Days*, *Stressproof Your Life*, or *The Complete Idiot's Guide to Overcoming Stress*. (There's another book in that series, incidentally, called *The Complete Idiot's Guide to Enhancing Self-Esteem*: is that the most self-defeating self-help title ever?) In later life, Selye recanted: his English had been poor, he said, and he hadn't meant to use the word 'stress' at all. What he meant was something more like 'strain'.[34]

The distinction matters. Because of how we use the word 'stress' colloquially – and how physicists use it, too – it brings to mind an external force: it implies that the problem is whatever things (stressors) are pressing on us from outside. 'Strain' is more faithful to Selye's intended meaning, which is that the problem lies in how we respond to those forces.

There's a certain comfort in thinking of stress as an external thing: it implies it's beyond your control, and so not your responsibility. It lets you feel busy, and may evoke sympathy; it relieves you of the obligation to change. But it also implies that the answer to reducing stress lies in avoiding that external thing. There's short-term relief in fleeing a stressful situation for a calm and peaceful one, but if the problem is really how we respond to 'stressful' situations, that won't leave us better off next time. We're assailed by lifestyle suggestions promising stress reduction: blissful holidays, say, or downshifting to the country. But if you're using them to avoid things that trigger your negative responses, mightn't it be wiser to work on your responses instead?

That's the question motivating the study of what psychologists call 'resilience', the characteristics that cause some to thrive amid what others think of as intolerable stress. Amanda Ripley's book, *The Unthinkable*, examines who survives when faced with natural disasters or terrorism, and who doesn't. It's largely a matter of beliefs: survivors are those who think they have some control over external circumstances, and who see how even a negative experience might lead to growth. Overconfident people, who overestimate their powers, do particularly well.

Changing your beliefs is no mean feat. But just knowing that that's where stress is really located is a good start. That's not an argument for putting up with an insane job, relationship or other circumstance. But it offers the possibility of making a choice – not getting submerged by stress, nor fleeing what triggers it, but doing what the Buddhist nun Pema Chödrön calls 'learning to stay'.

IN PRAISE OF EMBARRASSMENT

One reason it's hard to study emotions is that it's tricky to recreate them in a lab. Ever since university ethics committees started getting sniffy about inflicting psychological damage on members of the public, it's been bad form to induce, say, sadness by tricking people into believing a relative has died; researchers play gloomy music instead. (To induce happiness, they lamely hand out free coffee mugs, or £5 notes.) But embarrassment is an exception: it's easy to embarrass people, within ethics guidelines, by asking them to suck a dummy, or sing along to cheesy music, or by wiring a pyramid of toilet rolls in a supermarket so it collapses when someone passes, some of which experimenters have actually done.[35]

Yet none of their work has dispelled the fundamental weirdness of embarrassment. It's an emotion concerned with

mere social niceties, yet it's often overpowering. Memories of
mortification persist for decades; studies have found we'll go
to dangerous lengths to avoid it, skipping medical checkups,
having unsafe sex rather than buying condoms, even hesitating
to save people from drowning for fear of misjudging the
situation.[36] People 'underestimate how much they will allow
the threat of embarrassment to govern their own future
choices', argues the psychologist Christine Harris. 'We tend
to make choices that maintain a veneer of smooth social
interaction', even when they're hugely risky.[37]

Embarrassment, it was originally assumed, was a response
to breaking social rules. (Condom-buying and medical
checkups don't break rules, but may feel like they do.) But
then more and more research started to suggest that rule-
breaking wasn't required. Just being the centre of attention,
or being praised, was enough; people even got embarrassed
by things happening to others.[38] The discovery of 'empathic
embarrassment' caused a stir, but to us acute sufferers, it's old
news: we leap to change channels when Sacha Baron Cohen's
character Borat makes people look stupid, even when they're
racists who deserve it; at weddings, we cringe pre-emptively
during speeches, even if they're good. (This makes reading
embarrassment research difficult. I felt for the thief, pleading
not guilty and representing himself, who asked a witness: 'Did
you get a good look at my face when I took your purse?')

Why might an emotion largely associated with etiquette
breaches be so overwhelming? In his book *Born to Be Good*,
the scholar Dacher Keltner makes a powerful case that
embarrassment is evolution's answer to the 'commitment
problem': it's in everyone's interests to collaborate for long-
term gain, but how do you weed out the conmen who want
to take advantage? Perhaps because they're unembarrassable.
Embarrassment – signalled by facial microexpressions that can't

be faked and that are remarkably consistent across cultures – 'reveals how much the individual cares about the rules that bind us together'. In the moment you realise you've come to the restaurant without your wallet, your eyes shoot down, your head tilts, a smile flickers. These are 'the most potent nonverbal clues we have to an individual's commitment to the moral order,' Keltner explains. It's little solace, but your blushes keep society functioning.

HOW TO FEEL ALIVE

The word 'awesome', it's fair to say, has become devalued through overuse. In 2008, I was sitting in the press section at a political event when a young official approached and said if I didn't mind switching seats, 'that would be awesome'. (This was in the United States, admittedly, where the overuse is more extreme than elsewhere.) I switched. 'That's awesome,' he responded. I overheard him use the word several more times. I realise it's possible he was an endearingly unjaded chap, perpetually astonished by the human capacity for doing things such as moving from one chair to another. But I doubt it.

Real awe is harder to come by. Most of us lead 'awe-deficient' lives, according to the neuropsychologist Paul Pearsall, who died in 2007 and who argued that awe should be considered 'the eleventh emotion', in addition to the ten commonly recognised by researchers. If we don't realise we lack awe, perhaps that's because we understand it so little: even Pearsall struggled to define its strange mix of fascination and fright, which can be invoked by a landscape or a newborn baby, but also by a natural disaster or a cancer diagnosis. 'The best description I've been able to give it so far is that – no matter how good or bad our brain considers whatever is happening to be – it is feeling more completely alive than we thought possible before we were in awe,' he writes in his final book, *Awe: The Delights and Dangers of Our Eleventh Emotion*, which begins with the story of the near-death, in infancy, of his son. He'd never been unhappier than while waiting to learn if his son would survive, he said. But, 'at the same time, I have never felt such profound awe'.

The centrepiece of Pearsall's research was the 'Study of the Awe-Inspired', a mammoth investigation of people who felt awe regularly. Living a more awe-filled life, Pearsall concluded, wasn't about seeking happiness, but about feeling more intensely – higher highs, but also lower lows. 'If you want to be happy all the time, awe is not for you,' he observes. 'It's too upsetting and causes too much uncertainty.' Being that alive – that immersed in experience – is exposing; it involves not 'closure' but what he calls 'open-ture'. (Excessive happiness actually works against the state of growth and engagement psychologists call 'flourishing': the bizarrely precise conclusion of the researcher Barbara Fredrickson is that the healthiest ratio of happy to sad feelings is 2.9:1.[39] Sure enough, Pearsall found that those closest to that point reported the most awe.)

His book has a terrible twist. After Pearsall submitted the manuscript, he recounts in an epilogue, his son committed suicide, aged 35. Pearsall and his wife discovered the body. 'I am now writing in one of the most intense, deep, painful aspects of awe ... I know there won't be "closure" or "getting past" what's happened,' he writes. 'If I can stay in awe of what's happening, I won't expect answers. I don't want there to be [any] ... I want to yearn, grieve, and cry for our son for the rest of my life.'

And then, arrestingly, this phrase, which taken out of context might seem baffling: 'I feel more alive than I've ever felt.'

WHY TRYING TO MAKE LIFE FUN BACKFIRES

In *Zen and the Art of Motorcycle Maintenance*, Robert Pirsig's nameless narrator, travelling with his son, pulls up at Crater Lake in Oregon, a natural wonder of vivid blue water surrounded by sheer cliffs. The US National Park Service calls it 'a place of immeasurable beauty', but the narrator is underwhelmed: '[We] see the Crater Lake with a feeling of, "Well, there it is", just as the pictures show. I watch the other tourists, all of whom seem to have out-of-place looks, too . . . You point to something as having Quality, and the Quality tends to go away.'

I thought of that recently while in the Arctic, researching a magazine article. The trip was endlessly inspiring, with one exception: the northern lights. They'd been so hyped that by the time I was woken in the early hours and told to come outside and marvel, the moment was already spoiled. I was too busy monitoring my own amazement levels and finding them wanting. The northern lights: well, there they were.

The annoying thing about positive emotions – happiness, wonder, love – is that when you pressure yourself into trying to feel them, you can't. When the pressure comes from others, it's worse, which is surely part of the reason for the revulsion many employees feel in the face of desperate corporate efforts to 'make work fun'. One of the most popular business books on both sides of the Atlantic in recent years has been *Fish! A Remarkable Way to Boost Morale and Improve Results*, purportedly based on the high spirits of salespeople at Seattle's fish market, who fling fish through the air to each other as they work. Several major US firms have 'adopted the Fish! philosophy': employees are rewarded with 'fish cards' when they show the right attitude, and the very best workers get a soft toy fish called Pete the Perch thrown at them by colleagues. ('Play!' is one of four Fish! principles, because, in the words of one Fish! worksheet, 'everyone can benefit from a little lightening up during the day'.) Every time I think about Pete the Perch, something inside me dies. Has none of these fun-fixated managers ever watched *The Office*?

These attempts to induce good feelings through top-down effort are self-defeating, whether they're imposed on workers by management or imposed on yourself by your rational brain. There's something in the definition of happiness that requires that it arise freely; you can provide the right environment for it, but can't force the matter. Otherwise you (or those you manage) get caught in the psychological trap known as the double bind – the unspoken demand whereby, in the words of the philosopher Alan Watts, 'you are required to do something that will be acceptable only if you do it voluntarily'.

Enforced happiness is no happiness at all, even if the person doing the enforcing is you. Anyone who's ever gone on holiday with a grim-faced determination to Have a Relaxing Time knows this all too well: deciding to make yourself relax isn't going to help you relax – just like adding an exclamation mark to the title of your book isn't necessarily going to help make it fun. (There are some exceptions.)

WHY FORGETTING TO EAT LUNCH COULD ALTER THE COURSE OF HISTORY

Not long ago, the British Psychological Society asked some of the world's leading psychologists a rather personal question: having spent so much time trying to understand people, what was the one nagging thing they still didn't understand about themselves? One respondent was Norbert Schwarz, whose many contributions to the field include the finding that gloomy weather can make your whole life look bad. The incidental feeling that it induces colours your entire outlook, at least until you become aware that this is what's happening, whereupon the effect vanishes. 'You'd think I'd learned that lesson, and now know how to deal with gloomy skies,' Schwarz told the BPS ruefully. 'I don't. They still get me ... Why does insight into how such influences work not help us notice them when they occur?'

We can surely all empathise. I think of myself as generally happy, but every so often I'm struck by a fleeting mood of unhappiness or anxiety that quickly escalates. On a really bad day, I may spend hours stuck in angst-ridden maunderings, wondering if I need to make major changes in my life. It's usually then that I realise I've forgotten to eat lunch. One tuna sandwich later, the mood is gone. And yet, 'Am I hungry?' is never my first response to feeling bad: my brain, apparently, would prefer to distress itself with reflections on the ultimate meaninglessness of human existence than to direct my body to a nearby sandwich shop.

There are two frustrating aspects to this. The first, as Schwarz points out, is the forgetting: knowing there's a simple fix doesn't mean you'll remember it when you need to. The other is the extraordinary power of these transient states: though in truth they might signify nothing more than moderate hunger, or the fact that it's overcast, they condition how you feel about everything. In a study entitled 'After the Movies', some crafty Australian researchers grilled people leaving the cinema about their views on politics and morality; they discovered that those leaving happy films were optimistic and lenient, while those leaving aggressive or sad ones were far more pessimistic and strict.[40] (They tried to control for the fact that different kinds of people might choose different kinds of movies in the first place.) Alcoholics Anonymous, meanwhile, urges its adherents to memorise the acronym 'halt', for 'never too hungry, never too angry, never too lonely, never too tired', as a caution against the minor, everyday factors that can lead to dark moods, and thence to full-blown relapse.

'Life is a train of moods like a string of beads,' wrote Ralph Waldo Emerson, 'and as we pass through them they prove to be many coloured lenses, which paint the world their own hue, and each shows us only what lies in its own focus.' The implications of all this, if you think too hard about it, grow dizzying: how many wars have been started, rather than averted at the last minute, because someone was underslept? How many marriage proposals accepted because it was sunny, or because the view from the observation deck was so dramatic? How many momentous decisions taken, how many life-courses altered, for want of a tuna sandwich?

THE TRUTH ABOUT LONELINESS

'I remember the year eye contact stopped,' one man recalls in *Loneliness*, a book by the psychologist and neuroscientist John Cacioppo. 'It wasn't some big demographic shift. People just seemed to give up on relating to each other. Now this town is one of the loneliest places on earth.' That was in California. British people might protest that eye contact, which we've never been keen on, isn't a good indicator of connectedness. But loneliness is ubiquitous in the western world, and research suggests it's more than a bad feeling: lonely people get ill more, die sooner and do intellectual tasks less well.[41] One recent study found they even feel, literally, colder.[42]

The harsh irony, Cacioppo writes, is that loneliness renders us worse at forging the bonds that might relieve it. Hunger impels us to eat, and tiredness to sleep, but loneliness, which is a fear-based response to isolation, triggers hyper-alertness to further social dangers: we become less welcoming of friendly overtures. And as dieters fixate on food, loneliness prompts a fixation on the self, making things worse – one reason why volunteering promotes happiness (it's a distraction), and why books on making yourself more popular won't alleviate loneliness, even if they make you more popular.

The trouble is partly that we don't understand what loneliness is. When feeling it, we conclude we're dislikeable, lacking social skills or surrounded by unfriendly people. In fact, Cacioppo says, our genes and upbringing give us unique personal levels of vulnerability to the effects of isolation; we each have a different threshold for the connectedness we need in order to stay healthy. It works like a thermostat: much as physical pain serves as a warning, loneliness signals that we've fallen below our requirements. But we're terrible at reading our thermostats, so we flee claustrophobic towns for the big city, then regret it, or leave stifling jobs for self-employment, only to find that office life fulfilled a function we'd never realised. (It's also why every few years, craving solitude, I book a week's solo hiking in Scotland, only to discover that my tolerance for my own company lasts exactly three days.)

This solves a long-standing mystery of loneliness research: except at the extremes, people who report more loneliness don't have fewer friends; they don't spend more time alone; they're not less socially adept.[43] That seems bizarre – unless the reason for their loneliness is that they simply require more connection than others. A happy implication of Cacioppo's work is that loneliness needn't mean something's wrong with your social skills, just that you need a connectedness top-up. Deep friendships are best, but even a conversation at the shops helps. Feeling lonely from time to time 'is like feeling hungry or thirsty from time to time,' he writes. 'It is part of being human. The trick is to heed these signals in ways that bring long-term satisfaction.'

Jean-Paul Sartre, one imagines, would find this view lacking: it means that alleviating the feeling of being alone in the universe is no longer an existential challenge, but mere life-management, like exercising or drinking enough water. Still, I prefer the non-existential version.

THE POWER OF DANISH THINKING

The Danish word *hygge* (pronounced, very approximately, 'hooga') means something like 'cosiness', but with undertones of 'camaraderie' and 'wellbeing'. Denmark's tourist industry likes to suggest that it's untranslatable and unexportable: the only way to feel it is to hop on a plane to Copenhagen.

It's also a cherished part of the national character, which explains the uproar over a video released a while back by the tourism agency VisitDenmark – a cack-handed attempt at viral marketing in which an attractive blonde Danish woman claims to be trying to trace the father of her baby. 'You were on vacation here in Denmark . . . I was on my way home, and I think you had lost your friends,' she says. 'We decided to go down to the water to have a drink . . . I don't even remember your name . . . We were talking about Denmark, and the thing we have here, *hygge* . . . And I guess I decided to show you what *hygge*'s all about, because we went back to my house, and we ended up having sex. The next morning, when I woke up, you were gone.' The public outrage was instantaneous. Even worse than the implication that Danish women have loose morals, it seemed, was the misinterpretation of *hygge*.

Sex between two old friends could maybe, just about, be (to use the adjectival form) *hyggelig*. Impulsive, anonymous sex between strangers? Never.

Such are the perils of trying to translate the allegedly untranslatable. In fact, these days, linguists don't have much time for the idea that truly untranslatable words really exist. (Did you know the Inuit have 17 different words for 'tired urban myth about Inuit languages'?) But there are certainly words that aren't easily translated, and they frequently relate to feelings. Without the slightest bit of hard evidence, I've got to believe this makes a concrete difference to our emotional lives: if you don't have a readily accessible label for a feeling such as *hygge*, might that not help edge it out of your emotional range, or at least from the kinds of things you find time in your schedule to do? Our English talk about happiness is usually about pleasure, excitement or (occasionally) fulfilment. There are no English-language self-help books on *How To Live a Hyggelig Life*.

Hard-to-translate emotions aren't always positive, of course: the Portuguese *saudades* refers to a particular kind of longing, and the Korean *han* is a form of collectively felt resentment in the face of injustice, blended with lamentation. But the sense of cosiness embodied by *hygge* is especially interesting because something like it occurs again and again in non-English languages: the German *Gemütlichkeit* is somewhat similar, as is the Dutch *gezelligheid*; the Czech *pohoda* overlaps a little, too. There is, it seems, significant demand for this kind of friendly, secure, usually home-based warmth.

I've never really seen the appeal of cosiness of the English variety, because it seems so passive and lazy: apparently, I'm just not the sort to enjoy dragging the duvet to the sofa, making a cup of hot chocolate and bingeing on old episodes of *ER*. But *hygge*, a Danish friend explains, 'is a conscious activity. "Let's go to my house and cosy" – it doesn't make sense in English. But *hygge* is a verb as well as an adjective. It's something you do.'

That's more like it: not vegging out, but actively weaving the fabric of friendship and ease. There ought to be a word for it.

3

HOW TO WIN FRIENDS
AND INFLUENCE PEOPLE

Social Life

DALE CARNEGIE'S OLD-STYLE
RECIPE FOR SUCCESS

How to Win Friends and Influence People, the 1936 book that started the modern self-help movement, will be of particular benefit to you if you fall into any of the following categories: 1) You live in the 1930s; 2) You are a hard-working 1930s businessman looking to land that promotion, or show your appreciation of your wife, whose vocation is cooking your meals and helping you out of your 1930s coat each evening; 3) You are a hard-working 1930s businessman who doesn't yet have a wife but wants to ingratiate himself with a certain pretty 'salesgirl' at the department store where you buy your 1930s coats.

In other words, it's a bit dated. Yet, extraordinarily, Dale Carnegie's book continues to sell many thousands of copies every year, has never been out of print and, at the time of writing, is the eighteenth most popular self-help book on Amazon.com. The total number of copies sold is widely reported to have surpassed 15 million. Evidently, something about it still appeals strongly, so I thought I'd investigate.

'That's £7.99, please,' said the man in the bookshop. I muttered a thank you. Had I read the book, I'd have looked him in the eye, smiled and said, 'Thank you, Neil! I really appreciate your helping me today, Neil. Why don't you tell me a bit about yourself, Neil?'

Carnegie's rules for smooth social interaction and success in life involve never criticising other people openly, praising them at every opportunity, and 'becoming genuinely interested' in their jobs and hobbies, which is a laudable goal, except that in Carnegie's own examples it never amounts to anything more than pretending to be fascinated. 'Always make the other person feel important,' Carnegie writes. Oh, and: 'Remember that a person's name is, to that person, the sweetest and most important sound in any language.'

All this is either brilliantly empathetic, or coldly manipulative: I can't figure out which. Cigar-chomping captains of industry are saluted for keeping their workers productive through nothing but charm; the mining baron John D. Rockefeller is praised for subduing striking workers by making them feel wanted – as opposed to, say, increasing their wages. The truculent British part of my brain kept objecting to this as horribly fake, even as the other part pointed out that 'fake it till you make it' is a perfectly acceptable way of going about things.

The problem is not so much the initial fakery as the self-consciousness it induces. Watching yourself all day as you fine-tune your methods of interacting with people is a near-perfect way of driving yourself insane; eventually, you give up and slip back into living your life instead of watching yourself live it, at which point you revert to your natural temperament. Some have suggested my natural temperament involves an element of grumpiness. Usually, I'd reject this crossly, but having read Carnegie – who says you should never tell another person they're wrong – I'd like to say in response: 'You're right! That's fascinating. Now, tell me about yourself.'

I'M OK, YOU'RE FUNDAMENTALLY ANNOYING

It's a common observation, among residents and visitors alike, that to walk through London at rush hour is to encounter a staggeringly large number of rude people, angry people and aggressive people, many of whom are also stupid. The observation is so commonplace, in fact, that it presents a problem: if you've ever had cause to criticise London's obnoxious hordes, you've almost certainly been dismissed by someone else, at some point, as being one of the obnoxious types yourself. You're not, of course. You're a reasonable, warm-spirited person. You sometimes get irritable, after a stressful day, when it's raining and you forgot your umbrella, but who wouldn't? That doesn't make you an unpleasant person. It's other people who are irredeemably, intrinsically awful. (See also Sartre's famous remark that 'hell is other people, especially the ones who linger pointlessly at the cash machine for 45 seconds after withdrawing their money'.)

We think this way because we're hypocrites, certainly – but also thanks to one of the most important phenomena in social psychology, the fundamental attribution error, or FAE. In accounting for others' behaviour, we chronically overvalue personality-based explanations, while undervaluing situational ones. 'When we see someone else kick a vending machine for no visible reason, we assume they are "an angry person",' writes Eliezer Yudkowsky at the blog overcomingbias.com. 'But when you yourself kick the machine, it's because the bus was late, the train was early, your report is overdue, and now the damned vending machine has eaten your lunch money for the second day in a row. Surely, you think to yourself, anyone would kick the vending machine, in that situation.'

The bias runs deep. Few of us, surely, think of ourselves as having a fixed, monochrome personality: we're happy or sad, stressed or relaxed, depending on circumstances. Yet we stubbornly resist the notion that others might be similarly circumstance-dependent. In a well-known 1960s study, people were shown two essays, one arguing in favour of Castro's Cuba and one against. Even when it was explained that the authors had been ordered to adopt each position based on a coin-toss – that their situation, in other words, had forced their hand

– readers still concluded that the 'pro-Castro' author must be, deep down, pro-Castro, and the other anti.[44] (Intriguingly, this personality-trumps-situation bias seems less prevalent in more collectivist cultures, such as Japan, than individualist ones, such as America.[45])

Self-help gurus love to dispense personality-based counsel when it comes to others: there's advice for dealing with 'toxic people', 'energy vampires', the neurotic, the negative, the self-absorbed. Personality disorders do exist, to be sure, but the FAE suggests we should err on the side of cutting people some slack – that almost everyone believes that what they do, at any given moment, is a natural response to their circumstances.

There are broader ramifications, too. The FAE undermines arguments based on the idea of 'a few bad apples', whether that's torturers at Abu Ghraib or everyday criminals who are 'just born that way'. This isn't to excuse bad acts; it's simply being clear-eyed. 'While a few bad apples might spoil the barrel . . . a vinegar barrel will always transform sweet cucumbers into sour pickles,' notes Philip Zimbardo, in a paper entitled 'A Situationist Perspective on the Psychology of Evil'.[46] (Zimbardo's notorious Stanford Prison Experiment, in which students asked to play prison guards behaved with striking cruelty towards students playing prisoners, shows how powerful situational influences can be.) So, he wonders, 'does it make more sense to spend resources to identify, isolate and destroy bad apples, or to understand how vinegar works?'

WHY YOUR FRIENDS HAVE MORE FRIENDS THAN YOU DO

This is going to be awkward, but someone has to tell you, so it might as well be me: you're kind of a loser. You know that feeling you sometimes have that your friends have more friends than you? You're right. They do. And you know how almost everyone at the gym seems in better shape than you, and how everyone at your book club seems better read? Well, they are. If you're single, it's probably a while since you dated – what with you being such a loser – but when you did, do you recall thinking the other person was more romantically experienced than you? I'm afraid it was probably true.

The only consolation in all this is that it's nothing personal: it's a bizarre statistical fact that almost all of us have fewer friends than our friends, more flab than our fellow gym-goers, and so on. In other words, you're a loser, but it's not your fault: it's just mathematics. (I mean, it's probably just mathematics. You might be a catastrophic failure as a human being, for all I know. But let's focus on the mathematics.)

To anyone not steeped in the science of numbers, this seems crazy. Friendship is a two-way street, so you'd assume things would average out: any given person would be as likely to be more popular than their friends as less. But as the sociologist Scott Feld showed, in a 1991 paper bluntly entitled 'Why Your Friends Have More Friends Than You Do', this isn't true. If you list all your friends, and then ask them all how many friends they have, their average is very likely to be higher than your friend count.[47]

The reason is bewilderingly simple: 'You are more likely to be friends with someone who has more friends than with someone who has fewer friends,' as the psychologist Satoshi Kanazawa explains.[48] You're more likely to know more popular people, and less likely to know less popular ones. Some people may be completely friendless, but you're not friends with any of them.

The implications of this seeming paradox cascade through daily life. People at your gym tend to be fitter than you because you tend not to encounter the ones who rarely go; any given romantic partner is likely to have had more partners than you because you're more likely to be part of a larger group than a small one. ('If your lover only had one lover,' Kanazawa points out, 'you are probably not him.') This is also why people think of certain beaches or museums or airports as usually busier than they actually are: by definition, most people aren't there when they're less crowded.

This takes some mental gymnastics to appreciate, but it's deeply reassuring. We're often told that comparing yourself with others is a fast track to misery – 'the grass is always greener' – but the usual explanation is that we choose to compare ourselves with the wrong people: we pick the happiest, wealthiest, most talented people, and ignore how much better off we are than most. Feld's work, though, suggests that this is only half of the problem. When it comes to our social circles, the field from which we're choosing our comparisons is also skewed against us to begin with. So next time you catch yourself feeling self-pityingly inferior to almost everyone you know, take heart: you're right, but then again, it's probably the same for them, too.

ARE YOU AN ASKER OR A GUESSER?

The advice of etiquette experts on dealing with unwanted invitations, or overly demanding requests for favours, has always been the same: just say no. That may have been a useless mantra in the war on drugs, but in the war on relatives who want to stay for a fortnight, or colleagues trying to get you to do their work for them, the manners guru Emily Post's formulation – 'I'm afraid that won't be possible' – remains the gold standard. Excuses merely invite negotiation. The comic retort has its place (Peter Cook: 'Oh dear, I find I'm watching television that night'), and I'm fond of the tautological non-explanation ('I can't, because I'm unable to'). But these are variations on a theme. The best way to say no is to say no. Then shut up.

This is a lesson we're unable to learn, however, judging by the scores of books promising to help us. *The Power of a Positive No, How to Say No Without Feeling Guilty, The Book of No* . . . Publishers, certainly, seem unable to refuse. Such books are meant to help combat the 'disease to please' – a phrase that doesn't make grammatical sense, but rhymes, giving it instant pop-psychology cachet. There are certainly profound issues here, relating to self-esteem, guilt and more. But it's also worth considering whether part of the problem doesn't originate in a simple misunderstanding between two types of people: Askers and Guessers.

This terminology comes from a brilliant web posting by Andrea Donderi that has achieved minor cult status online.[49] We are raised, the theory runs, in one of two cultures. In Ask culture, people grow up believing they can ask for anything – a favour, a pay rise – fully realising the answer may be no. In Guess culture, by contrast, you avoid 'putting a request into words unless you're pretty sure the answer will be yes . . . A key skill is putting out delicate feelers. If you do this with enough subtlety, you won't have to make the request directly; you'll get an offer. Even then, the offer may be genuine or *pro forma*; it takes yet more skill and delicacy to discern whether you should accept.'

Neither approach is 'wrong', but when an Asker meets a Guesser, unpleasantness results. An Asker won't think it's rude to request two weeks in your spare room, but a Guess culture person will hear it as presumptuous and resent the agony involved in saying no. Your boss, asking for a project to be finished early, may be an overdemanding boor – or just an Asker, who is assuming you might decline. If you're a Guesser, you'll hear it as an expectation. This is a spectrum, not a dichotomy, and it explains cross-cultural awkwardnesses, too: Brits and Americans get discombobulated doing business in Japan, because it's a Guess culture, yet experience Russians as rude, because they tend to be diehard Askers.

Self-help seeks to make us all Askers, training us to both ask and refuse with relish; the mediation expert William Ury recommends memorising 'anchor phrases' such as 'that doesn't work for me'. But Guessers can take solace in logic: in many social situations (though perhaps not in the workplace) the very fact that you're receiving an anxiety-inducing request is proof that the person asking is an Asker. He or she is half-expecting you'll say no, and has no inkling of the torture you're experiencing. So say no, and see what happens. Nothing will.

HOW TO BE INTERESTING

Everyone would like to be thought of as interesting, but the quest is fraught with dangers. 'Before you read this discussion of how we can become more interesting,' wrote Barbara Wedgwood, in a 1965 book called *How to Be a More Interesting Woman*, 'think of this: not every man wants an interesting woman, any more than every husband wants or could even tolerate a beauty. It is a very difficult thing to be a woman.'

That particular consideration may be somewhat less pressing today, but learning to be interesting remains a very difficult thing, for men and women. Self-help books promise to show you how, yet usually end up parroting Wedgwood's comically counterproductive advice. For example: 'Find some subject that really interests you and become an expert in it.' We all know people like this, who won't shut up about their specialism. But we don't tend to describe them as 'interesting'.

The problem may be that nobody can define interestingness to start with. Consequently, many tips for cultivating it just restate the problem: 'Develop an instinct for the things people want to hear about.' Or they veer close to circular reasoning. 'Start a blog,' the designer and blogger Russell Davies recommends, but as experience shows, only interesting people – Davies included – start interesting blogs. Boring people's blogs are distillations of their boringness.

Interestingly – no, I promise – boringness in a conversation partner is much easier to define than interestingness. It is the refusal to grant equal status to your interlocutor as a person. 'There is no more infuriating feeling than having your individuality ignored, your own psychology unacknowledged,' argues Robert Greene in *The 48 Laws of Power*. Perhaps that's why bores provoke a level of rage that seems disproportionate to their offence. 'People do all kinds of aggressive and antisocial things to each other – surely I do a few myself – and talking on and on can't be the worst of them,' writes the literary scholar Mark Edmundson in *The American Scholar*. 'Still, being on the receiving end of such verbiage sends me close to the edge.'

Specialist-subject bores, Edmundson observes, aren't even the worst: the worst are those who think they're experts in *your* specialism. Of one colleague, prone to offering wisdom on Coleridge, he writes: 'He must think he's doing me a favour by lecturing me on a matter close to my heart, and I think I'm doing him a favour by listening. When two people take themselves to be doing each other favours when they're not, the account books get unbalanced and disaster is up the road, for each one thinks he has the other in his debt.'

All this may help explain why self-help's other famous tip
for becoming interesting – that it's all about being interested
in the other person – seems so insufficient. Certainly, it gets
at something true: we're all egotists, and pandering to that
can work. But being ostentatiously interested is still a form
of egotism, and asking all the questions is a way of controlling
the conversation. The technique of 'active listening' is a worthy
one, but try one iota too hard and you've swung the focus
back to yourself again. Especially if you're doing it only to
seem interesting. An alarming possibility rears its head: are all
attempts to become interesting inherently self-centred – and
thus prone to make you more boring?

THE MYSTERIES OF LOVE, SOLVED!

It's a time-worn observation that for every famous proverb,
there's an equal and opposite proverb – do many hands make
light work, or do too many cooks spoil the broth? So when
it comes to our notions of romance, it's baffling how long
the phrase 'opposites attract' has persisted as if it were fact.
The counter-proverb here, of course, is that birds of a feather
flock together. And if you must base your psychological outlook
on proverbs, aren't humans more likely to behave like birds
than like magnets? In recent years, several researchers have
shown that opposites don't attract.[50] Search for a date using
the 'scientific approach' of the leading site eharmony.com,
and you'll be matched with potential lovers based on various
commonalities that are 'predictors of long-term relationship
success'. Compatibility, then, is about similarity. Good. So that's
the eternal mystery of love finally solved. Right?

Well, no, and the complicating factor comes courtesy of Ted
Huston, a University of Texas psychology professor who runs

the PAIR Project, a long-term study of married couples that began in 1981. The project has reached numerous intriguing conclusions, such as that couples who are 'particularly lovey-dovey' as newlyweds are more likely to divorce – a finding that, I admit, triggers my *schadenfreude* response, having tolerated far too many ostentatious public displays of affection by such couples. But the project's most fascinating finding is detailed in Tara Parker-Pope's book *For Better (For Worse): The Science of a Happy Marriage*. Happy and unhappy relationships, Huston found, simply aren't much correlated with how many likes, dislikes and related characteristics a couple does or doesn't share. It's not that opposites attract, or that similar people attract; rather, he argues, the whole question of compatibility, in either of these senses, just isn't very important in the success or failure of any given romance. Which is head-spinningly confusing, when you think about it: how can the outcome of a relationship between two people *not* depend on what those people are like?

There's a way through this seeming paradox, but it requires that we rethink compatibility entirely. Huston argues that it does play one specific and unexpected role in love: when couples start worrying about whether they're compatible, it's usually the sign of a relationship in trouble. 'We're just not compatible' really means 'we're not getting along'. Seen like this, compatibility is just a label we put on the black box of love: when things are working out, we call it compatibility; when they're not, we blame incompatibility. The mystery of what makes relationships work hasn't been explained, only renamed.

Behind all this is a deeper assumption: that whatever it is that makes a pairing flourish is something each party brings into the relationship from outside. The psychologist Robert Epstein is on a lifelong mission to establish the opposite: that compatibility, if it means anything, is something built from *inside* a relationship, and that love can be consciously created. All that two partners need share, at the outset, is the willingness to try. Which all sounds like so much feelgood vagueness until you learn that, in 2002, Epstein met a woman on a plane and, in an effort to prove his point, persuaded her to try to fall in love with him.

Epstein's 'Love Project', which fixated the US media for several weeks, involved him and the woman, Gabriella Castillo, pursuing various techniques – affectionate touch, talking about their vulnerabilities, etcetera – that earlier studies had suggested would give rise to feelings of affection. And love did blossom, but let's be honest: it spoils the story that things didn't work out long-term. (The given reason, which sounds fair enough, is that Castillo lived in Venezuela, while Epstein lived in the US; the logistics were too much of a challenge.) Still, Epstein insists his basic point stands, and marshals studies to support it. Eye-gazing alone, according to his research, can cause leaps in feelings of affection of up to 70 per cent among people who barely know each other.[51] These days, Epstein studies arranged marriages (not to be confused with forced marriages) and cites evidence to suggest that, by and large, the love that grows within them is far more robust than in what we call love marriages.[52]

This needn't be an argument, if you're single, for asking your grandmother or favourite aunt to select your future spouse. But it strongly implies that love can be built with almost anyone willing to have a go – and that to spend years hunting for someone with compatible qualities is to get things backwards. Too much choice can paralyse us, encouraging the illusion that a 'soulmate' might be lurking out there when in fact, Epstein argues, soulmates are created. The blogger Tim Ferriss quotes one female friend, eager to find a partner:

'If I could only choose between three decent guys, it'd be a done deal. I'd be married already.' And probably happily married, too.

THE ABILENE PARADOX, OR HOW TO PLEASE NONE OF THE PEOPLE NONE OF THE TIME

I'm sure I can't be the only person who, as Christmas approaches, likes to draw the curtains, stoke the fire, fix myself a mince pie and a brandy, and curl up with the summer 1974 edition of the sociology journal *Organizational Dynamics*. Wait – I am the only person? That's a shame, because it contains an article that holds the key to the whole stress-inducing, sanity-threatening psychodrama that is Christmas. Bear with me on this.

The article is called 'The Abilene Paradox', and it's by the management theorist Jerry Harvey; it begins with a personal anecdote set not at Christmas but during a stiflingly hot Texas summer. Harvey and his wife were staying with her parents, and relaxing one afternoon when his father-in-law suggested a trip to Abilene, 50 miles away, for dinner. Harvey was appalled at the thought of driving 'across a godforsaken desert, in a furnace-like temperature . . . to eat unpalatable food'. But his wife seemed keen, so he kept his objections to himself.

The experience was as terrible as he'd predicted. Later, trying to be upbeat, he said, 'That was a great trip, wasn't it?' But one by one, each family member confessed they'd hated it: they had agreed to go only because they believed it was what the others wanted. 'Listen, I never wanted to go to Abilene,' Harvey's father-in-law said. 'I just thought you might be bored.'

Harvey's focus is on business: his point is that employees

are so scared of standing out that companies end up taking decisions that don't reflect the views of any of their members, 'thereby defeat[ing] the very purpose they set out to achieve'. His article and subsequent book became a management sensation. But the paradox seems just as applicable to the original organisation, the family – especially during holidays such as Christmas, with the added burden of expectations. How many long-standing traditions do you re-run during such times, when everyone involved would secretly rather not? For some families, presumably, the whole notion of getting together at Christmas is an example of the paradox: a ritual of strained nerves that everybody performs for everybody else's sake. I ought to emphasise that I'm not talking about my family. But then, according to the paradox, I wouldn't dare to admit it if I were.

This shouldn't be interpreted as a Scrooge-like condemnation of family togetherness, nor of traditions people genuinely enjoy. If anything, learning how to defeat the Abilene paradox – which you can really only do, Harvey concludes, by having the guts to speak up – is a strategy for improved relationships. (Maybe couples who take holidays separately are on to something, having had the courage to admit that's what they prefer?) We fret a lot about how to handle disagreement, but Harvey shows that agreement may sometimes be the real threat to our wellbeing.

So here's a real-life psychology experiment to try next time you're at a holiday gathering: if there's a family ritual you don't enjoy, try gently dissenting, and see what ensues. At best, you'll be rewarded with a chorus of happy relief. At worst, people will get tetchy. And they were going to do that at some point anyway, weren't they?

BREAK OUT OF THE ECHO CHAMBER

During the 2008 US presidential election, American friends would occasionally tell me that Barack Obama's victory seemed assured because they hadn't met one person – not one! – who planned on voting Republican. They were right about the outcome, of course. But about 58 million people voted against Obama; it was just that you didn't run into them in the coffee shops of Brooklyn. By the same logic, I conclude that nobody in Britain supports the death penalty, that everyone was obsessed with *The Wire*, and that almost no one read *The Da Vinci Code*. Opinion polls will back me up on this, provided they're conducted entirely among the clientele of north London gastropubs.

The faintly depressing human tendency to seek out and spend time with those most similar to us is known in social science as 'homophily', and it shapes our views, and our lives, in ways we're barely aware of. It explains why, if you know the political positions of a person's friends, you can have a very good guess at their own. It's also why, say, creationists imagine that the debate over evolution is an active and unresolved one: in their social circles, it is. We long to have our opinions confirmed, not challenged, and thus, as the Harvard media researcher Ethan Zuckerman puts it, 'Homophily causes ignorance.' (It also makes us more extreme, studies of 'group polarisation' indicate.[53] A group of conservatives, given the chance to discuss politics among themselves, will grow more conservative.) Even priding yourself on being open-minded is no defence if your natural, homophilic inclination is to hang out with other people like you, celebrating your love of diversity.

Technology risks making things worse: on the Internet, most obviously, it's possible to exist almost entirely within a feedback loop shaped by your own preferences. For all its faults, the era when everyone watched the same news bulletin at least exposed people to information they hadn't been looking for. When you Google for something, by contrast, you're imposing the severest of filters, right from the start, on what you'll permit into your field of attention. On sites such as Amazon and iTunes, homophily is a selling point: it's the basis for 'collaborative filtering', whereby you're recommended books and music on the basis of what others who made the same purchase – people like you – also enjoyed.

The unspoken assumption here is that you know what you like – that satisfying your existing preferences, and maybe expanding them a little around the edges, is the path to fulfilment. But if happiness research has taught us anything, it's that we're terrible at predicting what will bring us pleasure. Might we end up happier by exposing ourselves more often to serendipity, or even, specifically, to the people and things we don't think we'd like?

You don't need technology to do that, but then again, technology needn't be the enemy. Facebook could easily offer a list of the People You're Least Likely to Know; imagine what that could do for cross-cultural understanding. And I love the Unsuggester, a feature of the books site librarything.com: enter a book you've recently read, and it'll provide a list of titles least likely to appear alongside it on other people's bookshelves. Tell it you're a fan of Kant's *Critique of Pure Reason*, and it'll suggest you read *Confessions of a Shopaholic* by Sophie Kinsella. And maybe you should.

IT'S NOT ABOUT YOU

The great thing about developing some familiarity with the world of psychology, as I have done by now, is that whenever you're faced with one of life's challenges, you can easily call to mind some helpful piece of wisdom. Let's say, hypothetically, that you're crossing the road one autumn morning when some malicious halfwit of a taxi driver skids round the corner, douses you with puddle-water, damn near hits you, then speeds off. You don't need to become consumed with rage, swear loudly, and demand to know if he was trying to kill you. 'How interesting!' you can superciliously observe instead. 'If I were to get angry, that would be a classic example of "egocentricity bias" – the near-universal human error whereby we think of ourselves as the cause and target of others' actions far more than is actually the case! That driver wasn't trying to soak me, or kill me. Maybe it wasn't his fault he didn't see me. And even if he is a generally careless driver, which would be bad, it would be absurd to respond as if he had it in for me personally.'

Like I said, this is hypothetical. Personally, I go for the rage and swearing every time. But I shouldn't: many studies show that we're terrible at guessing what's really going on in other people's heads, and we habitually assume we figure far more prominently than we do.[54] If you're worried that your boss is displeased with your work, that your child does things just to spite you, or that your so-called friends are sneering at you behind your back, be reassured. It's not that these people are thinking wonderful thoughts about you – they're just not thinking about you at all. (Partly, no doubt, because they're too busy worrying about what others are thinking about them.)

The psychologist Thomas Gilovich once made students walk into college classrooms wearing a Barry Manilow t-shirt, after he'd already conducted a survey that showed they would find this particularly embarrassing. On average, the t-shirt-wearers estimated that 46 per cent of the other students noticed their horrific clothing choice; in reality, only 23 per cent did.[55] Anyone who's ever been a wallflower at a party knows this 'social spotlight effect' well: you stick out like a sore thumb, except that, actually, you don't. Gilovich speculates that evolution might have given us this acute self-consciousness because being aware of what others thought of us was once a life-and-death matter. It isn't any more, but our emotions haven't caught up.

An interesting implication of all this is that egocentricity isn't the sole preserve of the kind of people we generally call egocentric – people who think they're fantastic. Even if you're convinced that everyone hates you, you're still giving yourself far too prominent a role in the mental lives of others. From one perspective, this universal self-absorption seems a rather bleak state of affairs, but from another it's freeing: you don't need to worry about how you're perceived as much as you thought you did. Either way, it seems to be universally true, so you might as well embrace it.

I just feel a bit sorry for Barry Manilow. Only a bit, though; I've got my own problems to be worrying about.

DATING TIPS FROM THE EIGHTEENTH CENTURY

It goes without saying that many self-help books, perhaps almost all of them, fail to deliver what they promise. But there's a special subgroup that promises things you wouldn't want in the first place. Take *How to Date Paris Hilton*, by a former stripper named Clive 'Rock Solid' Webb, which is doomed from page one due to the author's failure to address the question of why, in the name of all that is holy, anyone would ever want to do that. (It turns out that 'Paris Hilton' is intended as a synonym for 'beautiful women', though the book is useless anyway, since Mr Webb – or should that be Mr Solid? – is accustomed to taking his clothes off in public, and thus presumably doesn't suffer from shyness.)

There are countless such titles on how to make yourself more likeable, in the context of dating, friendship, networking and so on. Most feel slightly manipulative and soulless, but they're one of the most venerable strands of self-improvement, reaching back to the eighteenth century – and to a man who, had he used Clive Webb's publishers, would probably have been known as Benjamin 'Kite in a Thunderstorm' Franklin.

Franklin is a curious bird: a witty writer, skilled diplomat and a genius who invented lightning conductors – and yet, one can't help imagining, slightly irritating. 'He seems like the type of guy,' writes Rita Koganzon in the American political magazine *Doublethink Quarterly*, 'who might have a lot of Facebook friends who, upon further questioning, would admit they accepted his friend request only because they didn't want to offend him.' But he also put his finger on a strange truth about human attraction: people like you more if they've done a favour for you than if you've done a favour for them. Franklin recalls trying to win over a hostile member of the Pennsylvania legislature, not by kowtowing but by asking to borrow a specific rare book from his library. The man obliged, and friendship flourished. 'He that has once done you a kindness,' Franklin concludes, 'will be more ready to do you another, than he whom you yourself have obliged.'

The Ben Franklin Effect, as psychologists call it, works

because we hate cognitive dissonance: we can't stand a mismatch between our actions and thoughts. So if we find ourselves helping someone out, we'll unconsciously adjust our feelings for them. After all, we don't want to feel we're valuing someone who doesn't deserve it. In one key study, students won money in a contest; afterwards, some were asked to return it because, they were told, it was the hard-up researcher's own cash. In a subsequent survey, that group liked the researcher significantly more than those who weren't asked to give any money back.[56]

The implications are striking. Don't suck up to your boss – make demands. Don't shower your friends with gifts – ask to borrow their stuff. And whatever Clive 'Rock Solid' Webb or other dating advisers might say, don't sidle up to members of the opposite sex in bars and offer to buy them drinks; get them to buy you drinks instead.

YOU DON'T KNOW YOUR FRIENDS AS WELL AS YOU THINK

I like my close friends a lot – that's the point of close friends, surely – and yet, on an almost daily basis, they appal me. I have a friend who thinks voting is a waste of time, and one who believes, sincerely, that musical theatre is a legitimate art form; I have another friend who treats any arrangement to meet at a given time and place as an amusing hypothesis, an approximation of something he might, or might not, actually end up doing. What's especially odd is that every time I encounter these traits, I'm shocked all over again.

It's generally held that friends are people with whom we choose to forge relationships because we find their specific personalities agreeable, or similar to our own, and yet experience regularly contradicts this. What is a friend, really? 'All that one can safely say . . . is that a friend is someone one likes and wishes to see again,' writes Joseph Epstein, fumbling for a definition in his book *Friendship: An Exposé*. 'Though,' he adds archly, 'I can think of exceptions and qualifications even to this innocuous formulation.'

The truth is that we don't know our friends nearly as well as we imagine. Research demonstrates that we tend to assume our friends agree with us – on politics, ethics, etcetera – more than they really do.[57] The striking part is that the problem doesn't appear to lessen as a friendship deepens: when the researchers Michael Gill and William Swann questioned students sharing rooms, they found that, as time passed, people became ever more confident in the accuracy of their judgments about the other, and yet, in reality, the judgments grew no more accurate.[58] Two people might become dear friends (or romantic partners), yet remain ignorant about vast areas of each other's inner lives.

This seems strange, until you consider, as Drake Bennett puts it in the *Boston Globe*, that 'many of the benefits that friendship provides don't necessarily depend on perfect familiarity; they stem instead from something closer to reliability'. Friendship may be less about being drawn to someone's personality than about finding someone willing to endorse your sense of your own personality. In agreeing to keep you company, or lend an ear, a friend provides the 'social-identity support' we crave. You needn't be a close match with someone, nor deeply familiar with their psyche, to strike this mutual deal. And once a friendship has begun, cognitive dissonance helps keep it going: having decided that someone's your friend, you want to like them, if only to confirm that you made the right decision. We don't want to know everything about our friends, Gill and Swann suggest: what we seek is 'pragmatic accuracy'. We don't

base friendships on what we learn about people; we decide
what to learn about people, and what to ignore, based on having
decided to be friends.

Perhaps this sounds chillingly narcissistic – friendship
exposed as a self-serving ruse in which it doesn't matter who
your friends are, so long as they agree to the role, presumably
for their own equally egotistical reasons. Or perhaps there's
something moving about the notion of friendship as an
agreement to keep each other company, overlook each other's
faults and not probe too deeply in ways that might undermine
the friendship. It's somewhat lacking in the eloquent proverb
department, but maybe a true friend is someone who doesn't
ask many awkward questions.

STAND OUT FROM THE CROWD – BUT NOT TOO MUCH

Back when I was being pumped full of 'careers advice', one
line of argument held that the best approach to job interviews
was to be memorable at all costs. I recall the tale of the fresh-
faced graduate arriving at an advertising agency with a goldfish
in a plastic bag, which he used to illustrate some tortuous
point about branding. One heard tell of would-be management
consultants firing toy guns from which messages unfurled on
a piece of fabric. The approach can't have caught on, however,
or else our financial and commercial institutions would have
been taken over by flashy types with flair and not enough
real, humdrum skills, and the economy would have collapsed.

Oh, wait.

We live in less flashy times now. But the call to be remarkable,
albeit in less preposterous ways, remains loud. Books with
titles such as *Pop!: Stand Out in Any Crowd* and *101 Ways to*

Stand Out at Work argue that being different is the key to thriving, while seemingly infinite numbers of personal development blogs urge readers to 'live a remarkable life'. In this sober, mercifully goldfish-free rendering, the point has some merit: being distinctive enhances your market value. And who can't appreciate the psychological benefits of making, and being recognised for, a unique contribution in life, rather than following the herd?

What's odd about our preoccupation with remarkableness, though, is how it coexists with its opposite. Most self-help books that aren't about standing out are about fitting in: making friends, finding a like-minded partner, or realising that negative experiences – sadness, worry, stress – are really rather normal. And social psychology is awash with evidence of how far we'll go for the payoff of being the same. (In Solomon Asch's celebrated groupthink experiments, for example, 75 per cent of participants were willing to disbelieve their own eyes when others in the room – actors posing as subjects – insisted that lines of wildly different lengths were actually the same.[59])

The truth – that we need to stand out and to fit in – has been codified, in recent years, as 'optimal distinctiveness theory'. We seem to crave the sweet spot between being too exceptional or too normal, and we're constantly adjusting our behaviour to find this ideal. When we feel suffocated by sameness, we'll strive to make our mark, but if we feel too lonely in our differentness, we'll rush to conform.

In other words, it's a balance. And yet our attitudes to specialness and ordinariness are anything but even-handed: we celebrate one and disdain the other. ('The mass of men lead lives of quiet desperation', Thoreau famously wrote, and however right he was, it's hard not to detect a trace of a sneer directed at the conformists.) So it's worth asking whether we should always be striving to be remarkable. Might some of us be better advised to get over our issues with being ordinary?

I'm not in the habit of taking advice on happiness from Philip Larkin, an incorrigible misery-guts, but his poem 'Born Yesterday', dedicated to a newborn baby, might serve as a useful corrective: 'May you be ordinary;/Have, like other women,/An average of talents:/Not ugly, not good-looking,/Nothing uncustomary/To pull you off your balance . . . /In fact, may you be dull −/If that is what a skilled,/Vigilant, flexible,/Unemphasised, enthralled/Catching of happiness is called.'

THE TRUTH BEHIND YOUR
FACEBOOK STATUS

The people to whom I'm closest are, I'm guessing, similar to those closest to you: they have good days and bad days; they're often upbeat but sometimes depressed; occasionally, they experience major crises; and when you get them talking, usually over alcohol, they'll almost all prove more insecure than they'd ever admit in public. But my casual acquaintances are a different story. Judging by their Facebook updates, their tweets, their sporadic group emails and our infrequent conversations at parties, their lives are one long sequence of breathtaking road-trips, beach holidays, perfect weddings, exciting new jobs and adorable new babies. They are, in short, monumentally aggravating, and I'd unfriend them in a trice, except that it would be even more aggravating to suspect them of having so much fun behind my back.

While it's conceivable that my friends and family are a particularly catastrophic bunch, the real explanation is surely obvious: it's only those with whom I'm most intimate who let me see the unvarnished reality. That's a timeless truth, of course, but there's a strong case to be made that these days it's worse than ever: thanks to Facebook and other social networking sites – and the frictionless ease of electronic communication in general – it's far easier to maintain weak quasi-friendships, and thus to hear the burnished versions of far more lives. 'In my trips back [home], I have been struck each time by the discord between people's Facebook lives and what they say in private,' writes the blogger Stan James, in a penetrating post at wanderingstan.com. 'On Facebook they have been on an amazing vacation . . . in person they confess that the vacation was a desperate attempt to save a marriage. On Facebook they have been to glitterati tech conferences. In person they confess they haven't been able to sleep for months.'

That happiness is relative – that we're made happier or sadder in large part by how we compare our lives to those around us – is one of the oldest findings in 'positive psychology'. As James notes, people have long made the error of contrasting themselves unfavourably to television stars, imagining they know them when all they really know is a carefully edited presentation. But with quasi-friends, it's worse, because they're people we've actually met; it's thus even harder to remember we're not seeing the full picture. It's like an unceasing stream of those Christmas round-robin letters, crowing about little Jessica's triumph in grade three tuba. And you can't even blame the quasi-friends: in the semi-public world of Facebook and its ilk, they're hardly going to reveal their disappointments and private sadnesses, are they?

Analogous problems of vantage-point crop up regularly. The much-studied 'impostor syndrome', for example, relies on the fact that you can never really know the self-doubt behind other people's achievements, only your own. The same goes for organisations: corporations and governments seem ultra-professional – until you get an inside view, whereupon they're revealed to be seat-of-the-pants operations where almost nobody knows what they're doing.

Not that quasi-friends are entirely bad. Sociologists have shown that 'weak ties' are as crucial to the flourishing of social networks as strong ones; more quasi-friends probably also means more job opportunities, and more chance of making real friends, or meeting the love of your life.[60] Perhaps all we need is some kind of technological fix, to display a message under every chipper status update, and as a permanent subtitle on numerous television shows: 'Don't forget: this person is barely holding things together.'

4

HOW TO RULE THE OFFICE

Work Life

WHY MEETINGS SHOULD BE ABOLISHED

Almost everyone hates meetings, and yet the idea of doing away with them is seen as revolutionary, or ridiculous. Jim Buckmaster, chief executive of the hugely successful website craigslist.org, has a simple policy – 'No meetings, ever' – but if you're a manager, you're probably already thinking of reasons why you couldn't do the same. An important recent book, *Why Work Sucks and How to Fix It*, proposes a total shift in how we think about office life, but one part is considered so startling, it's singled out on the cover: 'No meetings.' It has been reported that senior executives find at least half of all meetings unproductive.[61] Yet still they happen. 'Meetings,' writes the humorist Dave Barry, 'are an addictive, highly self-indulgent activity that corporations and other large organisations habitually engage in only because they cannot actually masturbate.'

Why Work Sucks and How to Fix It reports on an experiment undertaken at the US electronics chain BestBuy: a 'results-only work environment', in which staff could work where and when they liked, so long as their jobs got done. The first casualty was meetings. 'Why do we spend so much of our business life talking about the business we need to take care of?' the authors write.

There are several reasons why meetings don't work. They move, in the words of the career coach Dale Dauten, 'at the pace of the slowest mind in the room', so that 'all but one participant will be bored, all but one mind underused'. A key purpose of meetings is information transfer, but they're based on the assumption that people absorb information best by hearing it, rather than reading it or discussing it over email, whereas in fact it's been estimated that only a minority of us are 'auditory learners'.[62] PowerPoint presentations may be worse. The investigation into the 2003 Columbia space shuttle disaster, caused by a fuel tank problem, suggested that NASA engineers might have been hampered in addressing it sooner because it was presented on PowerPoint slides, forcing the information into hierarchical lists of bullet points, ill-suited to how most brains work.

The key question for distinguishing a worthwhile meeting from a worthless one seems to be this: is it a 'status-report' meeting, designed for employees to tell each other things? If so, it's probably better handled on email or paper. That leaves a minority of 'good' meetings, whose value lies in the meeting of minds itself – for example, a well-run brainstorming session.

Countless books advise managers on how to motivate staff. But motivation isn't the problem. Generally, people want to work; they gripe when things like meetings stop them doing so. Indeed, a 2006 study showed there's only one group of people who say meetings enhance their wellbeing – those who also score low on 'accomplishment striving'.[63] In other words: people who enjoy meetings are those who don't like getting things done.

HOW TO STOP PEOPLE BOTHERING
YOU AT WORK

Books from the 1970s on time management always make two key suggestions for how to stop people interrupting you when you're trying to work: close the door to your office, and get your secretary to screen your phone calls. This would be brilliant advice, except that the entire time I was working full-time in an office, I never had a door; I could have got my secretary to go and buy me one, but I never had a secretary, either. As a result, I was always extremely busy, and regrettably had no time to take what would have been the most cathartic action – i.e., hunting down and killing the person who first suggested that open-plan offices might be a boon to productivity.

Besides, trying to eradicate interruptions doesn't always make sense. Even more recent books counsel shutting yourself off from sources of distraction – *Never Check E-mail in the Morning*, by Julie Morgenstern, is one very readable example. But many of us these days work in jobs that behavioural scientists describe as 'interrupt-driven', where responding quickly to messages and requests is part of what we're paid to do: try telling a call-centre worker (or an investment banker, or a journalist) to take the phone off the hook for an hour. What we need are guerrilla tactics for managing office interruptions, and the personal-development gurus, of course, are happy to oblige:

1. Apply the 'two-minute rule'

This preposterously simple idea, from the productivity guru David Allen, really might change your life: deal immediately with all interruptions that you think can be dispatched in two minutes. (Write down the others, and process them later.) Crucially, two minutes is short enough not to lose a feel for the work you were engaged in. This is important, given the findings of the psychologist Mary Czerwinski, an 'interruption scientist' (no kidding): 40 per cent of the time, she notes, office workers who get distracted from a task don't return to it when the interruption ends.[64]

2. Use visual buffers to reduce face-to-face interruptions

A potted plant or stack of books on your desk need not literally block colleagues; people respond surprisingly sensitively to symbolic cues. I spent many days in the office wearing an outsized pair of headphones; amusingly, they can be very obviously plugged in to nothing at all, and you'll still be left alone.

3. Stop interrupting yourself

If surfing the web is a major source of distraction, adjust your browser's preferences so your homepage is 'Get Back to Work', by the blogger Mark Taw (marktaw.com/getbacktowork.htm), a page that a) tells you in very large letters to get back to work, and b) includes a clever system for clarifying and monitoring the work you're meant to be doing. By sharpening your awareness of what you're doing, self-monitoring of this kind can seriously reduce the time spent in the depressing limbo that is neither focused work nor real relaxation.

There are other techniques for stopping people bothering you. But they're not for the weak-hearted, and may have negative consequences for your social acceptability. Roquefort cheese. At your desk. That's all I'm saying for now.

WHAT COLOUR SHALL WE PAINT THE BIKE SHED?

The English writer C. Northcote Parkinson is best remembered for his maxim that 'work expands to fill the time available', but that wasn't his only biting observation about the irrationality and ridiculousness of business life. (Though, actually, if it really had taken him his whole career to come up with Parkinson's Law, that would have been an amusing demonstration of Parkinson's Law.) A less well-known but equally spot-on dictum, also outlined in his book *Parkinson's Law*, is the Law of Triviality, which he illustrates with an imaginary tale in which a firm's executives meet to discuss two new projects: an atomic reactor and a company bike shed. The reactor is complex and bewilderingly expensive, and non-experts risk embarrassment if they speak up, so it gets approved in two and a half minutes. But everyone knows about bikes and bike sheds, and everyone has an opinion. The bike shed, Parkinson writes, 'will be debated for an hour and a quarter, then deferred for decision to the next meeting, pending the gathering of more information'.

This has come to be known as the Colour of the Bike Shed Phenomenon: the time spent on any item will be in inverse proportion to its cost and importance. Relentlessly, the trivial squeezes out the non-trivial. The reactor may suffer a meltdown due to some overlooked technical matter, but never mind: check out the awesome letterhead stationery we spent so long getting right!

Parkinson's point – which also applies to politics and the media, where the focus, frustratingly, is often on the least important things – isn't simply that smaller matters are less intimidating to deal with. It's that when the members of any group are driven partly by personal egotism – as all of us are – their interests conspire, without them realising it, to keep the focus on the inconsequential. Each wants to demonstrate, to the boss or to themselves, that they are taking part, paying attention, making a difference, 'adding value'. But with complex subjects about which they're ignorant, they can't: they risk humiliation. They may also not want to dwell on their specialist subjects, preferring not to have the non-experts pry too closely. (In Parkinson's story, the nuclear expert keeps quiet: 'He would have to begin by explaining what a reactor is, and no one there would admit that he did not already know. Better to say nothing.')

So what gets discussed is precisely what doesn't matter.

'In Denmark we call it "setting your fingerprint",' notes Poul-Henning Kamp, a programmer who has helped popularise the conundrum, at the website bikeshed.com. 'It is about personal pride and prestige. It is about being able to point somewhere and say, "There! I did that . . . " Just think about footsteps in wet cement.'

Similar effects – where small stuff preoccupies us precisely because it's small – course through our lives. The Law of Triviality also calls to mind the caustic comment, usually attributed to Henry Kissinger, that 'academic politics are so vicious because the stakes are so small', which is surely a fair take on most office politics, too. I fear that something related is also what's transpiring whenever I get that delusional feeling of achievement from having powered through multiple unimportant items on my to-do list, leaving untouched the few tasks that really matter. Taken together, Parkinson's two laws amount to a wry but certainly not trivial warning: the work we do expands to fill the time available – and, half the time, it's not even the most important work.

THE SPECIAL BENEFITS OF NOT BEING A SPECIALIST

In the perfect society, wrote Karl Marx, nobody would be a specialist. It would be 'possible for me to do one thing today and another tomorrow – to hunt in the morning, fish in the afternoon, rear cattle in the evening, criticise after dinner, just as I have a mind, without ever becoming hunter, fisherman, herdsman or critic'. (The quote comes from his 1845 book *Theses on Feuerbach*, shortly to be republished, in a new translation by Paul McKenna, as *I Can Transform Your Capitalist Relations of Production in Seven Days*.) There's nothing particularly Marxist about this idea – you find it, also, in ancient Greece, and in the Renaissance – but where you don't find it is in the business section of your local chain bookshop. There, by contrast, the focus is on focus: defining your 'purpose', relentlessly pursuing your 'number one priority', and developing your 'personal brand'. Specialism rules.

The problem is that plenty of people don't have one number-one priority, even within the world of work. From an early age, we're taught to feel that this is bad, a mark of indecisiveness – a belief exacerbated not just by reading stress-inducing business books but by the very notion of a single, unitary 'career path'. 'The conventional wisdom [seems] indisputable,' writes Barbara Sher, whose excellent book *Refuse to Choose!* has made her the chief consoler of self-pitying generalists everywhere. The prevailing belief is that 'if you're a jack-of-all-trades, you'll always be a master of none. You'll become a dilettante, a dabbler, a superficial person – and you'll never have a decent career.'

Yet Sher identifies a specific personality type she calls 'scanners' and offers them a plethora of tips for flourishing in a non-scanner world. Another book, *One Person/Multiple Careers* by Marci Alboher, gathers examples of people who have made a success of what the author calls 'slash' careers. The unifying theme is how much damage is done by the mere belief, among generalists, that specialism is best. 'Almost every case of low self-esteem, shame, frustration . . . simply disappeared the moment they understood they were scanners, and stopped trying to be someone else,' Sher reports.

Apart from anything else, the 'one focus' belief serves to inhibit action: if you believe you have to give up your job as a lawyer in order to become a screenwriter – based on an underlying belief that people have to have one job – you'll probably never become a screenwriter. If you spend one hour actually screenwriting, you already are one.

Most of us, of course, have jobs to do, and a life outside our jobs to attend to; there's a limit to how much more we can cram in. But we can start by letting go of the idea that specialism is inherently superior. (In some fields, it's still better-paid, but Alboher marshals evidence that this is changing, too.) How strange that we should have persuaded ourselves that doing only a few of the things we can do is better than doing lots of them. As for that 'jack-of-all-trades' thing: the earliest published reference to Shakespeare – hardly an underachiever – as an actor and playwright refers to him using the Elizabethan equivalent of that term, 'Johannes factotum'.

Another famous dilettante: Leonardo da Vinci. I'm just saying.

THE (POSSIBLY NON-EXISTENT)
SECRET OF GREAT LEADERSHIP

Towards the end of his life, the great organisational thinker Peter Drucker sardonically observed that although he'd spent half a century speaking about the mysterious, seductive, much sought-after quality called 'leadership', he wasn't sure that there was much to be said about it at all. 'The only definition of a leader,' he remarked, 'is that a leader is someone who has followers.' This circularity hasn't stopped numerous gurus presenting themselves as purveyors of the 'laws' or 'secrets' of leadership. 'The true measure of leadership,' writes John Maxwell, who has published nearly 60 books on the topic, served as adviser to the US military and now runs a worldwide leadership development programme, 'is influence . . . If you don't have influence, you will never be able to lead others.' Um, yes, thanks.

Observations about the excretory habits of bears in arboreal settings may spring to mind, but that probably just shows you're not cut out to be a leader.

The more closely it's examined, the more 'leadership', good or bad, starts to look like a mirage. In his interesting book *Obliquity*, the economist John Kay cites John Sculley, chieftain of the Apple empire in the 1980s. (Another secret of leadership: lots of the people involved are called John.) Sculley's reign was a huge success until, suddenly, it wasn't: with profits in freefall, he was forced out. Much ink was spilled over this. Was he a great leader who lost his touch, or a mediocre one who'd briefly risen above himself? Kay suggests a third option: neither. Maybe Sculley just sat at the top while other forces – technological, economic, cultural – determined Apple's fortunes.

Kay quotes the philosopher Alasdair MacIntyre: 'One key reason why the presidents of large corporations do not, as some radical critics believe, control the United States is that they do not even succeed in controlling their own corporations . . . when implied organisational skill and power are deployed and the desired effect follows, all that we have witnessed is the same kind of sequence as when a clergyman is fortunate enough to pray for rain just before the unpredicted end of a drought.' That's extreme (and hard to square, say, with Steve Jobs's much more successful, and very personality-driven, reign at Apple). But it highlights the tautologies and rationalisations that abound. Even assuming that there are skilled and unskilled leaders, 'leadership' serves too often merely to re-label the mystery. See also 'charisma': it's all very well to describe Hitler, or George Clooney for that matter, as charismatic. But what have you really said?

Psychological studies support a related and similarly circular conclusion: the people we follow as leaders are the ones who decide they've got what it takes to lead. We chronically mistake bossiness for leaderly talent. Make the most suggestions in a group context, one research team found, and you're likely to be seen as the most competent, even if the suggestions are among the worst.[65] Voice an opinion three times over, another study suggests, and fellow group members are almost as likely to conclude it's the group's prevailing view as if three different people had voiced it.[66] ('Quantity,' Stalin supposedly said, 'has a quality all its own.')

None of which means there's no such thing as an effective leader. But trying to identify whatever it is that he or she does as some kind of essence called 'leadership' may raise more questions than it answers. What makes a great leader? A certain *je ne sais quoi*, of course.

I'M SORRY, I CAN'T DO THAT

It's entirely possible that you've never heard of strategic incompetence and yet that you are, at the same time, a lifelong expert at it. If you aren't, you'll know someone who is. Strategic incompetence is the art of avoiding undesirable tasks by pretending to be unable to do them, and though the phrase was apparently only fairly recently coined in a *Wall Street Journal* article, the concept is surely as old as humanity. Modern-day exemplars include the office colleague who responds to the photocopier message 'clear paper jam' by freezing in melodramatic pseudo-panic until someone else steps forward to help; you're equally guilty, though, if you've ever evaded a household task or DIY project by claiming you might screw things up. ('I'd do the laundry – I'm just worried I'll damage your clothes.') The *Journal* interviewed one executive who'd managed to avoid organising the office picnic for several years running. 'You'd be amazed,' he noted, 'at how much I don't know about picnics.'

What swiftly happens, the masters of strategic incompetence learn, is that people stop expecting you to undertake certain tasks; they no longer ask you to do them, and they adjust how they rate you: your failure to perform the activity stops counting against you. If all this sounds overly Machiavellian, it's worth noting that it's only a personalised version of what corporate types refer to as 'expectations management', which is a key component of any company's customer-relations strategy. If you want satisfied customers, it's certainly wise to act in ways that will satisfy them. But it's also wise to pay attention to (and, if possible, influence) their criteria for feeling satisfied.

Most of us are bad at this, because deep down we want to please people, whether in hope of personal gain or out of what the self-help writer Elizabeth Hilts calls 'toxic niceness': the chronic urge to please resulting from the fear of confrontation. I realise I'm not exactly part of the target market for her pop-psychology book *Getting In Touch With Your Inner Bitch* – she identifies toxic niceness as an overwhelmingly female phenomenon – but she's on to something, I think, that crosses gender boundaries. Seen from this perspective, expectations management isn't just for lazy people who want to avoid boring tasks. Training our bosses, partners or children not to expect a 'yes' in response to every single request might be crucial for preserving sanity.

If you start small, it's surprisingly easy to begin adjusting others' expectations. It's like strength training: gradually, you build up tolerance. If you think you shoulder an unfair burden of chores at home, pick one, don't do it, and monitor what happens. If you're driven crazy at work by ceaseless emails demanding instant responses, try always waiting a few hours to respond, even when you've no reason to wait. Far better to have a reputation as someone who reliably replies within 24 hours than someone who replies within seconds – because in the latter case, as soon as you fail to respond instantly, you'll be seen as underperforming. Thus do the people who try hardest to please end up annoying people more than those who don't try so hard. No, it's not fair. Well spotted.

HOW TO DRAW A LINE BETWEEN WORK AND LEISURE

It's probably true that we need a new word to describe the way that work, these days, seeps more and more into our free time, giving rise to an unfocused, dissatisfying twilight zone that's neither work nor leisure. Still, that doesn't excuse the American sociologist Dalton Conley, who has coined 'weisure' as a name for the phenomenon – a portmanteau of 'work' and 'leisure' that may be the most eye-searingly ugly neologism since 'vlogging' or 'Brangelina'. But 'weisure' is better than 'lork', I suppose. And unlike most other monstrous recent neologisms, it doesn't involve the words 'Twitter' or 'tweet'. So we should probably be thankful for small mercies.

As Conley notes, weisure isn't just a matter of mobile phones and BlackBerries enabling bosses to pester staff at all hours. It's also a subtler intermingling of worlds previously kept separate. We're more likely to make close friends through work than a generation ago, and less likely to work for monolithic organisations, which helped impose hard edges between downtime and time at work.[67] And judging by the explosion of books on the topic, we're doing far more networking – a concept that couldn't exist without a blurring of friendships and working relationships.

Self-help's prescriptions for combating the energy-sapping effects of weisure tend to focus on shoring up the dyke against the rising waters of work: switching off your mobile, say, or sticking with discipline to a strict going-home time. That's fine as far as it goes. But it ignores a less obvious dimension to the problem, in which the culprit isn't work, but leisure.

In its modern form, dating from Victorian times, leisure is a negative concept: it's defined in contrast to work, as non-work – the time we gain, as a result of earning money, that we don't need to spend earning money. (It sounds strange to refer to an unemployed person's free days as leisure time.) And so it's all too easy to think of it as 'empty' time – time, in other words, just asking to be colonised by work.

Many of us welcome in the invader. 'Most people reflexively say they prefer being at home to being at work,' writes Winifred Gallagher in *Rapt*, an absorbing book (appropriately enough) on the psychology of attention. But research into 'flow' – the state of mind when time falls away, and people feel 'in the zone' – suggests otherwise. 'On the job, they're much likelier to focus on activities that demand their attention, challenge their abilities, have a clear objective and elicit timely feedback – conditions that favour optimal experience,' Gallagher notes. At home, on the other hand, they watch TV, an activity that, according to one study, induces flow only 13 per cent of the time.[68] We crave leisure and disdain work even though it may be work, not leisure, that fulfils us more.

That's not an argument for workaholism. It's an argument, as Gallagher says, for 'pay[ing] as much attention to scheduling a productive evening or weekend as you do to your workday'. This feels wrong: we imagine that when leisure time finally arrives, we'll enjoy being spontaneous. Planning how to relax seems like a contradiction in terms. But then the moment arrives, and what we spontaneously decide is to watch TV, entering a half-focused, barely enjoyable state of passivity. Or, as I shall henceforth be calling it, 'peisure'.

THE WAR FOR YOUR ATTENTION,
AND HOW TO WIN IT

It's a reliable rule of life that any email marked 'urgent' – with a red exclamation mark, or a 'please read', or similar – can be safely ignored for days, and possibly for ever. A few of the people who send them are, presumably, self-important and do it all the time. But mostly it's a sign of insecurity: the sender knows only too well that their message is one you'd otherwise have every reason to neglect. That exclamation mark is a declaration of war. It says: I know better than you how you should apportion your attention to get your work done.

But 'urgent' emails are only the most obvious manifestation of an endemic phenomenon. The battle to decide what merits your attention at any moment is a constant, low-level war of all against all. You might believe it's always you who chooses what to focus on, or your boss. Yet in the average workplace, countless voices – superiors, underlings, clients, random emailers – compete to control your concentration. We complain of having too many things to do. But how much of that overworked feeling is really resentment that it wasn't you who got to decide those things were important?

This, the management guru Peter Drucker argued, is a distinctive problem of modern 'knowledge work'. When you're ploughing a field or shoeing a horse, the answer to the question 'What's the most important thing for me to be doing right now?' is usually obvious: it can't be fought over. Not so in the blurry world of ideas, hence Drucker's maxim that if you're a knowledge worker, defining your work – staying aware of what genuinely deserves your attention – is the most crucial work you'll do. This is why 'information overload' is a questionable complaint: if we couldn't handle vast amounts of information, we'd have a breakdown each time we stepped into nature, or a busy street. The real trouble is that we have defined too many things as worthy of having the power to distract us.

The best 'time-management' strategies are about reclaiming this power. Spending the first hour of the day (or more) on a major project before you check email is one example: that way, you start the morning by putting yourself, not the incoming flow of attention-demands, in the driving seat. Alternatively, make it harder for others to seize your focus: the website awayfind.com, for example, offers ingenious ways to make it slightly more laborious to email you on holiday, so people won't do so lightly.

The deeper truth is that in reality it's always you who's choosing what you're doing, though not in the straightforward way you might think. You're 100 per cent free to disobey a boss, refuse a task, quit a job; you have only to live with the consequences. It's always a choice. That's cold comfort, of course, if your choice is between doing appalling work and starving to death. But too often we live as if that's the case, when really, on closer inspection, it isn't.

THE TRIUMPH OF THE TALENTLESS

In 1969, a crotchety ex-schoolteacher named Laurence Peter published *The Peter Principle*, answering a question that millions, surely, had asked: why does the world contain so many people who are so strikingly useless at their jobs? Droll curmudgeon though he was, Peter's now-famous principle identified a real problem: in hierarchical organisations, people tend to rise to their 'level of incompetence'. Being good at your job gets you promoted, and so on, ever upwards, until your performance isn't good enough to warrant further advancement. Seen this way, it's no accident that companies and governments are filled with bunglers – they're giant machines for sorting people into precisely the jobs they can't do. The cartoonist Scott Adams offers the only marginally less depressing Dilbert Principle: modern corporations systematically promote their least talented staff to the ranks of management where, since managers don't really do anything, they're mainly harmless.

It's easy to see why you might accept a job despite knowing that it exceeded your capacities: better pay, prestige, unwillingness to admit your limits. But the problem of incompetence goes deeper. One of the hallmarks of being terrible at something, it turns out, is not realising how terrible you are.

The key study here is called 'Unskilled and Unaware of It', and assuming that the Cornell psychologists who conducted it weren't themselves unsuspectingly incompetent, its conclusions are unsettling. 'The trouble with the world is that the stupid are cocksure while the intelligent are full of doubt,' Bertrand Russell wrote. The Cornell study broadly concurs: those who scored worst in various tests requiring 'knowledge, wisdom or savvy' were those who most overestimated their performance; top achievers tended to underestimate.[69] A special version of this problem preoccupies the business scholar Michael Gerber, whose book *The E-Myth Revisited* ('e' stands for 'entrepreneur') makes a devastatingly simple case for why most small businesses fail. People assume that having a skill – baking, say – means they'll be skilled at running a business doing that thing, so they open a bakery. But there's no necessary connection; indeed, a keen baker is likely to find tasks such as book-keeping so aggravating, because they get in the way of baking, that he'll do them especially badly.

Even if you're fortunate enough to recognise your weaknesses, you may not respond wisely. According to Gallup research compiled by the marketing expert Marcus Buckingham, most people try to 'plug' their weaknesses, while the really successful focus on exploiting strengths.[70] The weakness-plugger is the employee who goes on courses to become less awful at public speaking, when she'd be better off in a job that calls on her written skills. But you'll rarely improve a weakness beyond mediocrity, argues Buckingham, not least because it's hard to invest sustained energy in something you don't enjoy. If you truly know what you're bad at, you're already ahead of the pack. Don't throw that away by wasting your time getting slightly less bad.

5

HOW TO GET MORE DONE

Productivity

THE CURE FOR PROCRASTINATION

In the summer of 2007, the world's leading experts on not getting things done gathered in Lima for the International Conference on Procrastination. No, I have no idea how long they'd been meaning to get around to it, and there will be no such smart-aleck commentary from me here: can you imagine how many incredibly lame jokes procrastination researchers have to endure on a daily basis? Peru was an apt choice: in March the same year, its government launched an initiative to combat the nation's chronic punctuality problem. (And, yes indeed, several officials did arrive late for a press conference to launch the campaign, according to a report in *The Times*.) But for all the scholarly research on 'task avoidance', and literally hundreds of self-help books, procrastination is still commonly misunderstood. Which means that if you suffer from it – and some people really do suffer – your attempts to cure it might be making it worse.

Chronic procrastination afflicts an estimated 20 per cent of Americans, according to the leading figure in procrastination research, Professor Joseph Ferrari, and the numbers are surely similar elsewhere.[71] But it isn't the same as laziness, being disorganised, or putting off boring chores. It's an active avoidance strategy, and because it's usually rooted in the fear of failure, or success, or loss of control, it most affects exactly those things that really matter to us, not the chores. Personally, I've spent many hours procrastinating by reading books and websites on combating procrastination – with the handy side-effect that I can summarise here what I reckon are the only three genuinely useful pieces of advice they contain:

1. Motivation follows action

Books on 'getting motivated', and hyper-energetic motivational speakers, ironically compound the problem by reinforcing the idea that you need to feel positive about doing something before you begin it. But that's a subtle form of pressure. What if you dropped the requirement of feeling good, accepted that you felt bad, and just started anyway? Motivation usually shows up quickly thereafter.

2. Resistance is a signpost

Resisting a task is usually a sign that it's meaningful – which is why it's awakening your fears and stimulating procrastination. You could adopt 'Do whatever you're resisting the most' as a philosophy of life. As Steven Pressfield says in his pompous but interesting book *The War of Art*, 'The more important [something] is to our soul's evolution, the more Resistance we will feel toward pursuing it.'

3. Schedule leisure, not work

Procrastination is an act of rebellion against what you believe you 'should' be doing, and mentally shouting at yourself to do it will only make you rebel more stubbornly. In his book *The Now Habit*, Neil Fiore suggests keeping an 'Unschedule' – a time log on which you make plans for leisure activities but on which you record hours of work only after you've finished them. If you plan in advance to do a certain number hours of work in a day, anything less becomes a failure; if you make no such plans, every minute worked counts as a success.

HOW TO EMPTY YOUR INBOX –
AND KEEP IT THAT WAY

Shut up and listen, because I'm about to share just about the only life-enhancement strategy I've managed to implement with near-complete success since starting this whole undertaking. Sadly, it's about keeping your email inbox under control, not how to have a fulfilling relationship or triple your income (I'm still working on those). But it has advantages, such as the envious comments you'll get from colleagues when they see the pristine whiteness of your inbox. 'You are a freak,' people tell me, with some regularity. That's got to be envy, right? Right?

Methods for managing information overflow abound, but it was one book and one website – David Allen's *Getting Things Done*, and 43folders.com – that facilitated my epiphany. The underlying principle is that your inbox shouldn't be a place to store emails: you wouldn't store regular mail on your doormat, and you wouldn't leave your groceries in shopping bags, returning to them to fish things out as needed. Yet that's how we treat email. Here's the alternative, in my own slightly remixed version:

Step 1. If you've got hundreds of emails hanging around from more than two months ago, move them into a new folder called something like 'my embarrassing backlog of emails'. It's unlikely there's anything in there so urgent it can't wait: someone would have pestered you about it by now. You'll return to this folder at some other point, for example never.

Step 2. Create a folder called 'archive'. If you already have a system for storing emails, move everything into this one.

You don't need to store emails according to who sent them, or what they're about: these days, any email program worth its salt can search the whole archive to locate something.

Step 3. Attack your inbox, email by email. If an email's useless, delete it. If not, ask yourself: is it 'active' – is there a specific action you, or someone else, needs to take, or do you just vaguely think it might be worth keeping? If the latter, move it to the archive. (Don't assume you have to respond to every email you're sent, either. Some just aren't worth it.)

Step 4. Now for the killer technique. Set an alarm for, say, 45 minutes, and starting from the top, address each 'active' email in turn, and determine the action required. If it can be done in a minute or two, do it. If not, write the action on a to-do list. Repeat the 45-minute trick as many times as you can bear – but you may be surprised at how much you'll get done in a single session. I was.

Step 5. If you've got a lot of emails relating to current projects that just can't be addressed in two minutes, consider printing them out and storing them with the rest of your papers for those projects. Remember to add any tasks that arise from them to your to-do list, as in Step 4.

Step 6. Bask in a well-ordered inbox. At most, it should now contain only those emails that a) are still 'active' and b) require a serious amount of your time. There's no trick for these – you just have to deal with them – but now, having weeded out the rest, you'll be able to focus on them exclusively. And perhaps reach inbox-emptiness. This might apply only to card-carrying productivity geeks, but there's something weirdly addictive about the blankness of an empty inbox which makes you want to keep it that way, by dealing with new emails promptly, not long after they arrive. If this last sentence makes you think I am psychotic, please pretend that you never read it.

THE ULTIMATE TO-DO LIST

I am astonished afresh each time I'm reminded that there are people who don't use to-do lists. They get up, do things all day, then go to bed. At no point in this process do they cross off tasks in a notebook, fill in timetables with coloured felt-tip pens, or organise complex systems of Post-its. They just do things. The notion of dedicating time to time-management strikes them as perverse – so presumably the idea of weighing the pros and cons of different kinds of to-do lists, as I've been doing recently, would trigger paroxysms of horror. Obviously, these people are weird and should be shunned. The ideas I'm about to discuss aren't for them.

For those of us who do keep a to-do list, whether sporadically or religiously, it's often a cause of mixed feelings. Writing a list provides you with a sense of control. But if you fail to complete it – or even end the day with a longer list than you started with, as sometimes happens – the feeling is one of defeat and of losing control. We use lists to help us focus, but then again, we value spontaneity; we don't want to feel governed by the list. We're also dimly aware that making lists can be a form of procrastination: you feel as if you're taking constructive action when really you're not.

Is there a way to use to-do lists happily, without adding stress or killing spontaneity? There's an absurd amount of writing on this topic, but only a handful of key points:

1. Don't use one list for multiple purposes
Are you using a single list both as a reminder of everything you're committed to doing, and as a menu of tasks for one specific day? That's a recipe for stress – plus, you'll never get

the buzz of crossing the last item off a list, which all true to-do list keepers treasure. So keep two: a 'master list', which you should never expect to 'finish', and a daily list, created by selecting tasks from the master list.

2. Use 'will-do', not 'to-do' lists

When making the daily list, don't pick 20 things you hope to do and that you think will add up to one day's work: you'll overestimate your capacities. Instead, pick the three or four most important things, and really commit to doing them, even if you think they'll take you only a couple of hours. Odd thought it may sound, keeping promises to yourself like this is exhilarating. If you find you have time to spare, pick more items from the master list.

3. The daily list should be a 'closed list'

New work floods in constantly, but don't add it to the current day's list unless it's an emergency: keep that list 'closed' and add the incoming items to the master list. Oh, and you know how you sometimes add a task to a list even though you've already completed it, just for the thrill of crossing it out? (Admit it: you do.) That's allowed. We tragic list-makers must take our pleasures where we can.

LOGGING YOUR LIFE

My favourite candidate in the American election of 2004 was Bob Graham, a Democratic senator from Florida whose policies were never very clear, but who had the endearing habit of logging every minute of his life in a series of colour-coded notebooks. '7–7.40 a.m.: kitchen, brew coffee, prepare and drink breakfast (soy, skim milk, OJ, peach, banana, blueberries)', read one typical entry. And another: '1.30–1.45 p.m. rewind *Ace Ventura*'. But this mild quirk counted against him – psychological quirks, or mild ones at least, apparently being a barrier to the presidency – and he soon dropped out of the race. This was a pity, since for anal retentives everywhere, Graham easily passed the legendary 'barbecue test' of US politics: would you invite this candidate round for a burger? ('7–7.45 p.m.: Attend barbecue.')

Graham's approach was overkill, to be sure. But logging certain aspects of your life can be a surprisingly powerful practice – not necessarily because there's much value in the record you create, but because the very act of recording exerts an interesting psychological effect. Spend a couple of days recording your time use in detail, several productivity experts advise, and you're likely to find yourself using it more efficiently. Record what you eat, and you'll find yourself eating more healthily, even without taking any other actions. (I tried both recently, for three days each. The time log alarmed me, by revealing how much time I'm capable of frittering away, but it helped, and the effects lasted beyond the three-day period. The food log turned me effortlessly into a health nut, but the effect was far more short-lived.)

This is an individualised version of the Hawthorne effect, observed in the 1920s and 1930s at a Chicago factory. Experimenters from Harvard tried to boost employee productivity by adding rest breaks of different durations, and by changing the lighting, temperature and other factors.[72] Many of the changes improved output – but so did changing things back. The mere fact of being observed, the experimenters concluded, was what made people behave differently. Copious doubts have since been raised about the study, and besides, it's easy to see how it could be used as an excuse for keeping workers under close surveillance. But as a personal technique, it seems to work, helping us make unconscious behaviour conscious.

The idea of making the unconscious conscious chimes with the Buddhist concept of 'mindfulness' – what the author and meditation teacher Sylvia Boorstein calls 'the practice of paying attention in every moment of one's day'. When I first encountered this notion, it was deeply unappealing: wouldn't it just mean becoming hyper-conscious of your every move, unable to relax because you were engaged in obsessive self-monitoring? The answer, I think, is that it could, if you did it in a judgmental way, relentlessly trying to analyse whether or not each action was the 'right' one. But the lesson of the 'personal Hawthorne effect' is that you don't need to make any such judgments. Merely observing your behaviour seems to make for better behaviour. Just paying attention is enough.

HOW TO HAVE IDEAS

Like many novelists, the sci-fi writer Neil Gaiman rarely does a public reading without being asked the tiresome question: 'Where do you get your ideas?' He used to respond facetiously – 'From a little ideas shop in Bognor Regis' – but that grew boring. 'I make them up,' is what he says now. 'Out of my head.' People don't like that. 'They look unhappy, as if I'm trying to slip a fast one past them,' he writes in an essay at neilgaiman.com. But the truth, he admits, is that he doesn't know where his ideas come from.

Through history, creative people have said the same, but that hasn't stanched the deluge of pop psychology books on how to generate ideas. The surprising problem with some of them is they are amazingly boring; *How to Have Creative Ideas*, by Edward de Bono, may contain useful advice, but, as with his other work, I've never had the perseverance to find out. (Hilariously, he once wrote a book non-ironically entitled *How You Can Be More Interesting*.) More often, they're plagued by a familiar, soul-destroying 'zaniness' of the same kind that inspires those team-building awaydays where managers play paintball and try not to ponder the futility of existence. One such is Doug Hall's book *Jump Start Your Brain: A Proven Method for Increasing Creativity by Up to 500%*. Hall runs workshops using the Eureka!® Stimulus Response™ method, so next time you have a eureka moment, best ask his permission.

It's tempting, amid this nonsense, to conclude that creativity is intrinsically mysterious and can't be elucidated. But what if we're just approaching it wrongly? 'Blue-sky thinking', like its cousin 'outside the box', has been mocked into obsolescence, but the metaphor they embody persists. We think of creativity as unrestrained and wild – that if we take the lids off our imaginations, great ideas will bubble up. We talk of 'unleashing' creativity. But the counter-argument, increasingly influential in business, is that creativity thrives on constraint.

'Is there something in the nature of constraints that brings out the best creativity?' wonders Scott Berkun, whose absorbing online essays on innovation, at scottberkun.com, are well worth reading. Consider a good haiku or sonnet, and the answer is obviously yes: it's precisely the limits of the form that inspire new ways of working inside them. In the workplace, that means no more open-ended brainstorming: if you want the best answers to a question, focus it narrowly; consider a time limit, too. Google reportedly sometimes puts fewer engineers on a problem than it needs, in an effort to inspire ingenuity.

The blue-sky metaphor further implies that ideas come from nowhere. But every idea is a combination of others, Berkun notes. 'Say it five times ... Every amazing creative thing you've ever seen [can] be broken down into smaller ideas that existed before. An automobile? An engine plus wheels. A telephone? Electricity plus sound . . . If you want to be a creator instead of a mere consumer, you must see ideas currently in the world as . . . ingredients waiting for reuse.'

So the pressure's off. You don't have to launch yourself into blue sky, nor conjure ideas from thin air. In fact, you almost certainly won't succeed if you try.

THE AMAZING POWERS OF
KITCHEN TIMERS, PART ONE

In 2006, an expert from the Oxford English Dictionary declared 'lifehacking' to be one of the words of the year. Getting nominated by the OED is usually a sign that a trend is already horribly past its prime, but lifehacking has won me over. The term, coined by web guru Danny O'Brien, comes from computing, where a 'hack' is a quick and dirty solution to a programming problem. Hence 'lifehacks': crude but ingenious productivity tricks for getting more done with less stress. The most compelling lesson I've learnt from the geeks is this: buy a kitchen timer. Recently, I've been carrying one almost everywhere I go – which is fine in all contexts except at airport security, where, for some reason, they seem suspicious of things that tick backwards towards zero.

Lifehackers love kitchen timers because they're cheap and simple tools, and you can use them in myriad ways to trick your brain into behaving how you want it to. Here are some uses:

1. Attacking daunting work tasks
Procrastination stems partly from terror – the longer a project languishes unfinished, the more horrifying it gets. The

productivity expert Mark Forster, in *Get Everything Done*, recommends diving into such dreaded work for timed 'bursts' of five minutes. That's a tiny, unintimidating amount of time. Also, crucially, this technique replaces a scary yardstick for measuring your progress ('I need to do this project really well!') with a neutral one ('I just need to work on this for five minutes').

Once you get into the swing of this, Forster suggests, start increasing the timed periods to 10 minutes and upwards. (A timer that doesn't tick audibly is probably best.)

2. Racing against the clock

For chores that aren't scary, just boring, set the clock for much less time than you think you'll need, then move fast. If you apply this to housework, you'll resemble a ridiculous stop-animation cartoon, but who's watching? My investigations suggest that a small city flat belonging to a feckless single male can be cleaned this way in under 20 minutes. You may object that you, in contrast, are the parent of four children, each with a psychological disorder that compels them to tear hundreds of sheets of paper into bits, mix them with Lego and flour and water and tread them into the carpet of every room in the house. Fine: you'll need more time. But the point is that you'll need less than you think. Try 25 per cent: if it looks like a four-hour ordeal, set the timer for 60 minutes.

3. Spending less time in the office

Evolution has built our brains to believe that things that are scarce are automatically more valuable. Make this work to your advantage, if your job allows it, by experimenting with a radically curtailed workday. If you had only four hours in which to work, how much more of that four-hour period

might you devote to working? Surveys keep suggesting that
the average office worker barely manages a handful of hours
of real work in a day.[73]

4. *Boiling eggs*
Unconventional, I know, but why not?

WHY EVERYTHING TAKES LONGER THAN WE
EXPECT, EVEN WHEN WE'RE EXPECTING IT TO

Hofstadter's law, conceived by the cognitive scientist Douglas
Hofstadter, goes like this: any task you're planning to complete
will always take longer than expected – even when Hofstadter's
law is taken into account. Even if you know a project will
overrun, and you build that knowledge into your planning,
it'll simply overrun your new estimated finish time, too. We
chronically underestimate the time things take: that's why
Sydney Opera House opened 10 years later than scheduled,
and why the new Wembley stadium in London opened in
2007, not in 2003, 2005 or 2006, each of which had been, at
various points, the predicted completion date. It's also why
the list-makers among us get up each day and make to-do
lists that by the same evening will seem laughable, even insane.

This is the 'planning fallacy', and it's been well-documented
by psychologists. (Presumably their experiments took much
longer than intended.) It's a strange kind of delusion, since
we're not really deluded. We *know* everything always takes
longer than expected; we just seem to forget, again and again.
In one study, students were asked when they expected to
complete an essay, and gave an average answer of ten days
before deadline. The reality was an average of one day before
deadline. Yet when the students were asked when they normally

completed such essays, they knew the truth: one day before deadline.[74]

It would be good to find a way around the planning fallacy, since never finishing your to-do list is a joyless way to live, and underestimating task-times means constantly rushing to finish things. (I speak as an expert.) How, though? Intuitively, it feels sensible to work out in detail what your projects involve, to break them into chunks and estimate how long each part will take. But the problem with unforeseen delays is you can't foresee them, no matter how finely detailed your planning. And so, writes Eliezer Yudkowsky at overcomingbias.com, the unlikely trick is to plan in *less* detail: to avoid considering the specifics and simply ask yourself how long it's taken to do roughly similar things before. 'You'll get back an answer that sounds hideously long, and clearly reflects no understanding of the special reasons why this task will take less time,' he writes. Nonetheless, 'this answer is true. Deal with it'.

Better yet, where possible, avoid planning altogether. Use the 'ready, fire, aim' approach, and correct your course as you go along. The major advantage is that you'll quickly start getting real feedback. If you're starting a new business, say, you won't have to imagine how customers might respond to your adverts; you'll know. This approach also helps when it comes to that curious category of tasks that don't obey Hofstadter's law: the ones you fret about for weeks, but that end up taking ten minutes. Sometimes, the secret to getting things done is just to do them.

THE OBSCURE PLEASURE OF INDEX CARDS

A few sentences from now, I'm going to reveal that I am obsessed with index cards, and you're probably going to mock me. That's OK; I can cope. But first let me just remind you of the company I'm in. Vladimir Nabokov wrote several novels on index cards. The celebrated nonfiction writer John McPhee has developed a whole system of research and writing around them, and Ludwig Wittgenstein reportedly used them to develop the *Tractatus Logico-Philosophicus*. Which means that index cards played a critical role in modern literature, journalism and philosophy. (And, incidentally, in the French Revolution, which some say was when they were invented: the new government used the backs of playing cards to record details of the books held in libraries seized from private ownership.) Impressive, no? All right. We can proceed.

I am obsessed with index cards.

A number of us, actually, suffer from this condition. For several years, a back-to-basics camp among productivity enthusiasts has embraced the unassuming index card as an unrivalled tool for personal organisation – a dirt-cheap, portable medium for keeping lists, taking notes, brainstorming, memorising, organising your schedule, or leaving reminders for yourself. One of their passions is the 'Hipster PDA' – a tongue-in-cheek proposed replacement for personal digital assistants, consisting of a stack of cards, a bulldog clip . . . and nothing else. But on the Internet, if you look for them, you can find photographs of some far more complex, borderline alarming efforts to organise one's entire life on index cards.[75]

To get theoretical for a moment, the cards fulfil two requirements of any good information storage system. First, it's easy to put stuff in: I'm far less likely to record a thought if I have to fiddle with a tricksy handheld electronic device. Second, it's easy to manipulate stuff once it's in. You can't, by contrast, endlessly rearrange the pages of a notebook in order to prioritise tasks, structure a piece of writing, discard things you no longer need, etcetera.

But might the power of index cards be greater still – mysterious, almost? I've wondered this ever since reading Robert Pirsig's novel *Lila*, in which the lead character is a philosopher who lives on a boat, writing his magnum opus on thousands of cards. As each thought occurs, he records it. Then, for hours, he rearranges the cards, grouping similar ideas together until a structure begins to emerge, seemingly independent of his will. This kind of 'emergent order' is a hallmark of the web – think Wikipedia – but it's somehow spookier when it happens on paper, and involves only one human.

The German sociologist Niklas Luhmann did something similar in reality, creating what he called his 'secondary memory': an index-card system that held, eventually, a lifetime of research notes. He came to think of it not as an archive but as a collaborator: as in *Lila*, an order emerged from the bottom up, and when he followed cross-references through the system, he'd discover connections that took him by surprise. Since being able to surprise someone is a characteristic of true communication, Luhmann argued that he was actually communicating with his system. Personally, I don't talk to my index cards. But maybe it's only a matter of time.

THE ONE PRETTY USEFUL INSIGHT
OF HIGHLY EFFECTIVE PEOPLE

I haven't yet felt the need, in this tour through popular psychology, to praise Stephen Covey, author of the famous *The 7 Habits of Highly Effective People*. It's one of those hopelessly unrealistic books that insists you begin your journey to fulfilment by Discovering Your Values and Finding Your Life Purpose – a process which, it's implied, will take a few days of slogging through several grim chapters of homework-style exercises. But a few days is both too long (who's got a few days to spare?) and too short: surely discovering your 'life purpose' takes your whole life? I finally lost respect for Covey when he decided there was an eighth Habit, requiring a new book. Who's to say there won't be a ninth, tenth, eleventh? I'm no maths expert, but I'm guessing the possibilities are, well, infinite.

But Covey's obsession with values leads him to one key insight, and it's all in that word 'effective'. People sometimes misremember the title as *The 7 Habits of Highly Efficient People*, but there's a reason why it's not called that. Covey recognises that there's no point being really good at doing stuff – highly efficient, in other words – if it's not the right stuff. Efficiency isn't the same as effectiveness. Work is probably where we misunderstand this the most. A day when lots gets done feels like a day well spent, regardless of what got done, and few companies manage to avoid the curse of 'presenteeism', where just being at your desk looking busy is rewarded. (Almost every time-management book falls into the trap of assuming that whatever you're doing is worth doing, and just needs doing more efficiently.) But there's 'busywork' in our personal lives, too, whenever the volume of activity becomes a stand-in for its value: what else is happening, really, when you go speed-dating, or push your kids into doing 25 extracurricular activities, or lead a frenetic social life based on keeping in touch with as many people as possible?

The scariest part – for an inveterate to-do list maker like me – came in Paul Graham's essay, *Good and Bad Procrastination*, at paulgraham.com. Graham identifies 'type-B procrastination': not inactivity, but unimportant busyness. 'Any advice about procrastination that concentrates on crossing things off your to-do list is not only incomplete, but positively misleading, if it doesn't consider the possibility that the to-do list is itself a form of type-B procrastination,' he writes. It's still procrastination, he points out, to do a lot of pointless tasks just because it feels nice, while the big, difficult thing – the one that matters – goes undone. I recognised myself and felt caught red-handed.

Of course, our lives are full of duties we don't find fulfilling but cannot just abandon in favour of more 'important' things. One popular piece of advice is to spend even just five minutes each day on one important thing, before the urgent stuff takes over. Increasingly, little tricks like this strike me as far more useful than grand philosophies of happiness. Meanwhile, if you find my life purpose, please get in touch.

HOW TO KILL TIME CREATIVELY

There's a popular subgenre of books about writing known informally as 'writer porn', in which famous authors describe their daily routines, which pens they use and, especially, the secluded mountain-top cabins where they work each morning for six blissfully undisturbed hours. I don't think I've ever actually met such an author, but for anyone whose job is even slightly 'creative', they stir envy: we'd all love such big chunks of time in which to focus. Instead, our lives are plagued with what the blogger Merlin Mann, at 43folders.com, calls 'interstitial time' – small chunks of minutes spent waiting at the doctor's surgery, or for someone who's late, or for a meeting postponed at short notice.

It feels like time wasted. But it needn't be. The poet William Carlos Williams, for example, wrote much of his oeuvre on the backs of prescription pads during gaps in his workday as a paediatrician. Here are some insights from bloggers and authors on using interstitial time, condensed into a form you can digest in three minutes, while waiting for that delayed train:

1. Don't fall for the 'major project' fallacy

Really important things, we tell ourselves, deserve big blocks of time and undivided concentration – so they never get done. In truth, most 'major projects' won't be any worse for being worked on in short bursts. As for those that will, remember G. K. Chesterton: 'If a thing is worth doing, it is worth doing badly.' Would you rather do something only fairly well, or die before you've done it at all?

2. Batch your tasks

You'll fit more into a sliver of time if you're doing several similar tasks – answering a stack of emails, say – than if you try to switch between different kinds of activity. Workplace studies show that time spent 'task-switching' eats up the day.[76] Even if your lifestyle does allow long, uninterrupted work periods, batching routine tasks is still sensible: deal with all your email twice daily, for example, and you'll spend less time on it overall.

3. Take inspiration from knitters

Mann praises knitting, which fulfils the three criteria of a good interstitial-time activity: it's portable, it can be done amid distractions, and even a few seconds spent on it contributes to the end result. (That's not the case with tasks requiring 'set-up', such as waiting for ever while Windows boots up on your laptop.) Identify in advance which of your tasks fit the knitting criteria: those involving reading and (hand)writing are a good place to start. Or take up knitting.

4. Do nothing, but do it deliberately

You don't have to use interstitial time to cram more activity into every last minute. But if you want to use it to 'stop and smell the roses', you have to choose to stop. The practice of meditation, some Buddhist teachers suggest, can be condensed into these fleeting moments. In any case, from a certain perspective, a sequence of fleeting moments is all we ever really have anyway.

AGAINST PRIORITISING

The back cover of *How to Get Control of Your Time and Your Life*, first published in 1973, featured this question, in big red capitals: 'What do Gloria Steinem and IBM have in common?' The answer was that both had sought the advice of the author, Alan Lakein, 'the world's leading expert on personal time management'. Nor was Lakein's influence limited to feminism and computing: his system, he boasted, had worked wonders for banks, oil companies, Neil Diamond, and the producer of the musical *Hair*. As if that weren't sufficient endorsement, Lakein also gets a glowing mention in Bill Clinton's autobiography. And there's a man who managed his time as president in such a way as to – well, to enable him to engage in numerous activities.

There's plenty of wisdom in Lakein's book, which is still in print. But at the core of his system, and many others since, is an approach I'm starting to suspect may be less smart than it looks: prioritisation. List your tasks and label them A, B or C depending on their importance, Lakein advises, then proceed accordingly. (It gets more complex: 'Label the most important of these A–1 . . . ') Some version of this remains central to how some firms try to encourage staff efficiency; many life coaches, meanwhile, recommend picking one 'life area' and prioritising it for a month or year. Yet, though I'm a tragic geek when it comes to tinkering with personal organisation systems, I've never made prioritising work. I used to think the problem was me. Now I'm less sure.

Intuitively, prioritising feels appealing. We're all too busy; we all waste time on urgent-but-unimportant stuff; we like the idea of deciding to address things in order of importance instead. But what does it really mean to make something a B-priority? If it needs doing, it needs doing. 'How impressed would you be,' wonders the personal development writer Mark Forster, at markforster.net, 'if your new car didn't have wing mirrors because the factory thought the engine was more important than the wing mirrors?' And if something's unimportant, why aim to do it at all?

You might respond that some things would just be nice to do if you got the time, but that's a red herring. You won't get the time – you're too busy, remember? – and if something is truly nice, it doesn't deserve relegation to B-status. (Advocates of prioritisation often implicitly equate 'unimportant' with 'fun', as if fun weren't hugely important.) Prioritising life areas is odder still. It makes no sense to rate, say, being a good parent as 'more important' than being healthy or financially secure; they're interdependent and, like apples and oranges, not comparable.

Ultimately, prioritisation is an avoidance strategy, fuelled by the illusion that the right system might somehow create more time, and that you might never have to confront the truth – which is that if you've got too much to do, you're going to have to find ways to reduce, not just reorganise, your to-do list. Since I enjoy few things more than reorganising my to-do list, this is rather annoying.

HOW TO BE A BETTER MORNING PERSON

Recently, I've been trying to become a Morning Person, and one of the unexpected benefits is this: it makes other Morning People a lot less irritating. I'm still unsettled by those 'day in the life' articles, according to which no successful entrepreneur, artist or politician ever gets up after 5 a.m. (Leonard Cohen, 2.30 a.m.; Dolly Parton, 3.30 a.m.; Warren Buffett, 5 a.m.; Condoleezza Rice, 4.30 a.m.) Broadly speaking, though, there's no better cure for peppy colleagues at 8.30 a.m. than becoming one, and you won't be surprised that the self-help world is bursting with advice on how to do it:

1. Don't try to sleep before you're tired

Some experts claim routine is everything – that you should sleep and rise at exactly the same time each day. Others insist you should listen to your body, sleeping from when you're tired until you wake naturally. The personal development blogger Steve Pavlina, at stevepavlina.com, argues they're both half right: the trick is to listen to your body in the evening – don't go to bed until you feel you could drift off in 15 minutes – and to your alarm in the morning. If you're accustomed to going to bed at 2 a.m., and set your alarm for 6 a.m., you'll have a few tired days at first. But you'll start turning in earlier, naturally adjusting your sleep time to what you really need.

2. Play tricks with your alarm clock

Hardcore disciplinarians just need to remember to place the clock across the room before retiring. Others can buy Clocky, an ingenious device that lets you snooze for up to ten minutes, then wheels itself off until it finds a place to hide, where it carries on beeping.

3. Take walks at dusk

If you're happy with the hours you're spending in bed, but just wish they started and finished earlier, you need more light at both ends of the day, according to the psychiatrist Daniel Kripke. Exposing yourself to fading light will prepare your brain for coming sleep.

Alternatively, though it's unpopular advice in self-improvement quarters, you might consider giving up. You'll rise earlier as you get older anyway. And besides, half of those overachievers who claim to rise at 3.30 a.m. may be lying. Several years ago, Kripke attached motion-sensors to his subjects and found that none of the people who claimed to be up at 4 a.m. actually were.[77] Using the methods above, I've been getting up regularly at 6 a.m., which is early enough for me. Assuming I'm telling the truth.

THE JOY OF FILING

I'm a Virgo. No, wait! I promise I'm not about to get all astrological on you – credulousness must have its limits. But the problem with being a Virgo who's convinced that horoscopes are nonsense is this: I really am a Virgo, character-wise. Those born under most signs get to be brave or loving or wise; Virgos get to be 'neat and tidy'. I bear my burden stoically: after all, it can't be everyone's destiny to win wars, or set hearts aflame, otherwise who'd be left to line up all the pens at a precise right angle to the side of the desk? I have some non-astrological theories on this – about Virgos being the oldest kids in their school years, and feeling responsible for keeping things orderly. But the point is that I am a neat-freak, and it's only right to acknowledge this before leaping into the topic – delightful to me, but maybe not to you – of filing systems.

Of course, it isn't just neat-freaks who use filing systems: we all have some way of organising our email, bank statements, office files, books and CDs, even if our chosen method is 'in a stack on the floor'. At work, many of us have to grapple with systems created by others. But what makes the subject so uninteresting to non-neat-freaks, I think, especially to people who pride themselves on being 'spontaneous', is that filing things away is a question not just of effort, but of effort with no clear payoff. Cooking a meal, putting up shelves: these require work, but at least the benefit is tangible. Spend 30 minutes putting your credit card bills in chronological order, as many books on 'getting organised' would have you do, and it might, one day, save a few seconds. But it might not. So we try, then we lose heart, instead creating that testament to self-deception, the 'to file' file.

But neither the neat-freaks nor the spontaneity-lovers are quite right. On the one hand, a good filing system will help, not hinder, spontaneity. When your brain trusts you'll be able to find things when you need them, you let go of trying to keep a mental handle on where everything is, freeing your head for creativity. On the other, almost all filing systems are indeed pointlessly laborious. Here's a middle way, which includes some borrowings from the productivity bible *Getting Things Done* and numerous blogs:

1. For paper files, a simple A–Z system is best. If you like, keep a list of filenames on computer, for easy searching.

2. For electronic documents, you really don't need to worry about a detailed filing system: as with your email archive, any decent computer can search it all, lightning-fast.

3. The degree of orderliness should be proportional to the likelihood of needing to locate things. Some documents might theoretically prove crucial, but probably won't ever be needed; throw them in a box and forget them. Don't bother imposing order on the mess until they're required – if they ever are.

4. File less; discard and recycle more. If you probably won't need a document – a magazine article, say – and could probably find it online, why keep it? Heretically, it's even worth considering junking books: if you could buy them again in an emergency, might you benefit more from the freed-up space?

THE AMAZING POWERS OF
KITCHEN TIMERS, PART TWO

Self-discipline, as human virtues go, is a pretty bloody annoying one. It has a pinched, goody-two-shoes, pleasure-denying air about it; it is the voice of the moralising teacher, or of the right-wing newspaper commentator who prescribes it as a remedy for every social ill but whose private life, one suspects, is a quagmire of neurosis and self-hate. Put it this way: you don't look forward to a big party at the weekend because you've been told all the self-disciplined people are going to be there. And yet – this is the annoying part – it's arguably by far the most important quality to cultivate. With enough of it, most desirable things (fulfilling relationships or work, happy moods, lots of money) are attainable; without it, none are. Even a committed hedonistic life requires plenty of self-discipline: you need it even to book the flight to Bali, to obtain those recreational drugs, or to arrange the circumstances for wild sexual encounters. Otherwise inertia will out, and you'll end up on the couch, half-dressed, watching reruns of

Antiques Roadshow and eating baked beans. I speak, as ever, from experience.

It's with all this in mind that I've been testing the Pomodoro Technique, a productivity method that its originator, Francesco Cirillo, has been teaching for ten years, but that has spawned a serious fan following only recently. (It's online at pomodorotechnique.com.) Adherents use words such as 'godsend' to describe its effect on their ability to focus. In truth, it's unmiraculous, but then so are most genuinely useful things.

Here's what you do: you pick a task, then set a kitchen timer for 25 minutes, no exceptions. Cirillo uses a kitchen timer shaped like a tomato, and is Italian, hence '*pomodoro*'. Do your work. When it rings, stop for five minutes. Repeat three more times, then take a longer break. That's just about it. Yet it works.

Half of all those reading that last paragraph will blink in confusion: 'Why do you need a technique? Why can't you just do stuff?' But the rest of us know that such tricks can be hugely effective, slowly strengthening the self-discipline muscle. They are, literally, tricks: the ticking clock takes an internal desire to get something done and fools some part of the brain into thinking it's external, that the clock must be obeyed. (Stopping dead at 25 minutes also creates useful momentum for starting again five minutes later.) Even the hokey language – Cirillo calls each 25-minute period a '*pomodoro*' – helps the process, by making the time-blocks seem like 'things', out in the world. Another geeky productivity scheme with an online following, Autofocus (markforster.net/autofocus-index), achieves something similar using cleverly structured to-do lists to 'force' the user to confront the tasks they've resolutely been avoiding.

The illusion, which we voluntarily swallow, is that choice

has been removed – and that there is now something stopping you from simply choosing to abandon your focus and default to whatever inertia would have you do: daydream, websurf, beerdrink. Some people take this too far, establishing inner dictators who yell at them all day, sapping the joy from life. Judiciously applied, though, this mental trickery is too useful a resource to ignore. Our brains are so easy to fool that it's borderline embarrassing; you might as well salvage some self-respect by exploiting that fact.

6

HOW TO USE YOUR BRAIN

Mental Life

ADVICE FROM THE MEMORY MASTER

Ben Pridmore, at the time of writing, is the world's highest-ranked competitive memoriser. In 2006, he recalled the sequence of a shuffled pack of playing cards after looking at them for exactly 31.03 seconds. That set a new record, beating the previous year's 32.13 seconds, which would have been bad news for the previous record-holder, except that that was Ben, too. If you need help memorising playing cards – or historical dates or lists of random numbers – Ben's your man. 'Yet the only thing anyone ever asks me about,' he told me, 'is how to remember people's names. And, personally, I'm terrible at remembering names.'

I've never understood why people get quite so embarrassed at forgetting others' names, but for many the issue seems to be a pressing one. Systems for remembering them (and other facts) make up a huge subsection of the self-help world. There are websites, workshops and audio tutorials; in the UK, the niche is dominated by another world memory champion, Dominic O'Brien, whose books include *Never Forget Names and Faces*, *How to Develop a Brilliant Memory Week by Week* and *The Amazing Memory Kit*.

What makes matching a name to a face so hard is that the possible ranges of names and faces are both effectively infinite. For sequences of numbers – even though numbers, of course, actually are infinite – it's different, at least if you have a memory like Ben's. 'All you have to do is turn each combination of two or three digits into a picture, so you just need a list of several thousand images,' he said, making it all sound rather easy. 'So, 166054137 becomes a catapult, launching at a soldier with an insect on him.'

Remembering a large number of names connected to faces

requires a different approach. Suggestions abound: Tom Weber, who calls himself The Memory Guy, advocates a version of the picture method: if you meet someone called Barbara, he tells people at his memory workshops, 'think of a barbed-wire fence. Now picture her wrapped in barbed wire.' I suppose so. But how do you remember which of the people you met is meant to be the one wrapped in barbed wire? Another approach is to use a name frequently the moment you learn it: 'Great to meet you, Tim. Glad to hear it, Tim.' This has the benefit of making you sound like a timeshare salesman, thus reducing the size of your social circle and, accordingly, the number of names you'll have to remember.

One surprising finding in the psychology of memory is that you're more likely to remember details of an event if you adopt the physical position you had at the time, which could work for name recall, if you meet people in a sufficient variety of positions.[78] Failing that, you'll have to resort to tricks. My favourite is to fail to introduce two people, then, a few seconds later, apologise for the oversight and hold out your palms, as if encouraging them to introduce themselves to each other. They will.

Ben is working on what sounds like my kind of self-help book. It's provisionally entitled *How to Be Clever* and it's 'about how to convince people you're a genius when you're not, by doing things like memorising lists of dates and playing cards. I don't claim to help you be a better person. I'm just claiming to help you get a reputation as a smart aleck.'

WHY MONEY MESSES WITH OUR HEADS

Let me introduce you to a man with the splendid name of T. Harv Eker, who wants to teach you how to become very wealthy indeed. He's founder of the StreetSmart Business School, which is similar to Harvard Business School or London Business School, except in one or two minor respects you don't need to worry your pretty little head about. He also runs a course called 'The Millionaire Mind', which, in common with much of the self-help literature on getting rich, is about inculcating the 'abundance mentality': the idea that money is limitless, and that it's your cosmic right to have plenty of it flow into your bank account.

Sadly, I can't reveal too many specifics, since 'The Millionaire Mind' costs $1,295 per person, and I'm still mired in the 'scarcity mindset'. For Harv, you'd have thought this might pose a problem – how to persuade people to pay lots of money, when their whole motivation is that they want, but don't yet have, lots of money? But it doesn't seem to have denied him a client base. Ignore news stories about declining fertility rates: there's still one born every minute.

Harv is right about one thing, though: we do have some strange ideas about money, and they get in the way of happiness. Studies show we'd prefer a smaller pay rise that left us better off than those around us, rather than a big one that everyone else received, too.[79] We're made much sadder about losing £100 than we are made happy by a £100 windfall.[80] And we put cash into savings accounts, yet simultaneously maintain credit card debts at higher rates of interest. These behaviours make no sense to traditional economists, since money is meant to be fungible: every pound is interchangeable with every other pound. But we don't treat it like that: we use 'mental accounting', dividing money into imaginary piles, then attaching emotional meaning to each.

A classic study of this phenomenon presented people with a question: if you paid $10 for a theatre ticket, then lost it, would you buy a new ticket? Only 46 per cent said yes. But what if you'd lost $10 in the street: would that stop you buying a ticket? This time, 88 per cent said they'd buy one, even though the loss was the same.[81] Many respondents, the experimenters said, felt that buying a second ticket would be eating too far into a fixed (but unspecific) amount they'd earmarked, almost subconsciously, for entertainment. Similarly, we're more likely to travel across town to save a small sum on a stapler than to save the same amount on a 42-inch plasma-screen TV. It doesn't seem worth it in the latter case, even though the benefit is identical.

Fortunately, you can turn this to your advantage. Blogger Bryan Fleming, at bryancfleming.com, has devised a philosophy of savings based on the observation that putting aside one dollar (or pound) each day is, at least for the moderately well-paid, pain-free: we write off expenditures that tiny as an inevitable part of daily living. Ramp it up incrementally, goes the theory, and you can adjust to spending far less without ever noticing. Or pay $1,295 to learn the secret of wealth – and if you do that, do tell me what it is.

WHY TIME SEEMS TO PASS
AT DIFFERENT SPEEDS

I came across a heart-stoppingly scary piece of research the other day, and ever since, like the Ancient Mariner, I've felt compelled to go around telling others, as if that might somehow ease the pain. Now it's your turn to hear it. We all know that time seems to speed up as we grow older – but according to studies at the University of Cincinnati in the 1970s, this effect is so pronounced that if you're 20 today, you're already halfway through life, in terms of your subjective experience of how time passes, even if you live until you're 80. And if you're 40

– again, assuming you live to be 80 – your life is 71 per cent over.[82] Basically, if you're older than about 30, you're almost dead. Have a great day!

It's not just ageing that meddles with our experience of time. A week-long holiday in a strange country seems, in retrospect, to have lasted much longer than the average work week, which flashes by. On the other hand, a desperately boring day seems to stretch infinitely. 'Put your hand on a hot stove for a minute, and it seems like an hour,' Einstein is supposed to have said. 'Sit with a pretty girl for an hour, and it seems like a minute. That's relativity.'

So can we 30-something geriatrics, and others, find a way to slow down time, to stretch our more enjoyable hours, without – like Dunbar in *Catch-22*, desperate to prolong his life – deliberately trying to keep ourselves bored? The psychology writer Steve Taylor offers some hope in his book, *Making Time: Why Time Seems to Pass at Different Speeds and How to Control It*. Partly, he accepts, time seems to speed up simply because each new year of our lives is a smaller proportion of the whole: if you're 10, any previous year of your existence was 10 per cent of your entire life; if you're 70, it was only 1.4 per cent.

But a more interesting idea, first volunteered by the grandfather of psychology, William James, is that time passes more slowly when we have to absorb more information. That would explain why it seems to take longer to get to a new destination than to return from it, and why a holiday seems longer than a week in the office. One obvious solution, therefore, is to seek newness, to break your routines. People who go on adventurous trips, Taylor writes, report longer-seeming holidays than those who choose the regularity and inactivity of a week on a beach.

Hang on, though: isn't time meant to fly when you're

enjoying yourself? Yes, but there's a confusion here, between the perception of time as we recall it in memory versus the experience of the moment itself. We don't usually want the hours to feel as if they're passing slowly: that's boredom. Rather, we want to look back on, say, the past year, and not feel as if it raced by. Our happiest times are those when we stop thinking about the passage of time altogether – but that we later remember as having lasted a deliciously long time. Extreme sports, meditation or any high-concentration activity will induce this effect. But sitting alone in a darkened room, whimpering about the implications of that terrifying Cincinnati research, will not. So I'm going to try to stop.

CAN YOU EVER REALLY KNOW YOURSELF?

'Know thyself,' was the phrase inscribed over the temple that was home to the Oracle at Delphi, which sounds a good prescription for living wisely and well. (A bit vague, sure, but that's oracles for you – always with the vagueness.) It wasn't until the past century that psychologists brought their pesky experiments to bear on that advice, whereupon they ran into a problem: we are, it seems, incapable of knowing our own minds. We think we know what's happening inside our brains – what makes us happy, or why we hold certain beliefs – but in truth, we don't: we're strangers to ourselves. Take physical attraction: in one recent experiment, participants were shown two pictures of women and told to pick the more attractive. Then they were given the picture and asked to explain their choice. Yet even when the researchers used sleight of hand, and started surreptitiously handing over the wrong picture, many still tried to justify their 'choice'. They'd refer, say, to a pretty pair of earrings, even though the woman they originally chose hadn't been wearing any.[83]

It seems so stupidly obvious that we should have a superior grasp of our own minds – we've got the perfect vantage point inside our own skulls, haven't we? – that it's painful to face the reality: our relationship to ourselves is more like that of an amateur psychologist, guessing at what's happening in there, with little more accuracy than if we were guessing about someone else. In 1977, when the academics Richard Nisbett and Timothy Wilson trawled the archives, they found this demonstrated in studies time and again. One classic case: stop people in a shopping centre and ask them to choose between four 'different' products that are really identical, and they're much more likely to choose the one on the farthest right, or the one they see last. Suggest that such factors influenced their choice, however, and they'll scoff.[84]

Think about this too much and it's liable to get depressing: it sounds like an argument for giving up on managing our internal lives, or on making certain choices over other ones in the quest for a fulfilling existence. If we don't know what we want, or why, then why make choices at all? Why not let yourself be buffeted by circumstance, carried along by the current of events, if it's as likely or unlikely as anything else to prove enjoyable?

Or perhaps a healthy appreciation for the limits of self-knowledge – for knowing what we don't know about ourselves – isn't such a defeatist attitude. Perhaps it could loosen us up. After all, once our fixed beliefs about what we need in order to be happy (in a relationship, say, or our work) are revealed to have such shaky foundations, isn't that a recipe not for resignation, but for experimentation? For doing things we'd written off as 'not really us' and discovering new depths to ourselves in the process? Oscar Wilde, who knew a thing or

two about destabilising fixed beliefs, had no truck with the
Oracle. 'Only the shallow know themselves,' he retorted.

SHOULD YOU TRUST YOUR BRAIN,
OR YOUR GUT?

In 1838, Charles Darwin took out his notebook and made
two lists that have since become famous. One was headed
'Marry', the other 'Not Marry': they were his attempt to
analyse, methodically, the pros and cons of seeking a wife.
'Charms of music and female chit-chat,' he wrote under
'Marry', and 'someone to take care of house'. The downsides
included 'loss of time' and 'perhaps quarrelling', but on balance
he seemed pro-marriage. 'Picture a nice soft wife on a sofa
with good fire and books . . . compare this vision with the
dingy reality of Great Marlborough Street,' he wrote. And:
'Better than a dog, anyhow.'

Darwin concluded that he should marry, and a year later
he did so. (He married his cousin – an intriguing decision
for an evolutionary theorist, but that's another story.) There's
something alienating about Darwin's lists, though – something
repellent about using ultra-rational methods to make such an
emotional decision. Even for less weighty dilemmas, there's
lots of evidence – popularised in Malcolm Gladwell's book
Blink – that we're better off relying on gut feelings. That can
be true even when there's an objectively 'right' answer: in one
experiment, people asked to choose the best equipped of
several cars were more often wrong when asked to analyse
their reasoning than when they judged intuitively.[85]

But gut-based decision-making has its own problems: what
if you're carried away by a passing mood, or overlook some
crucial bit of information? Psychologists and others suggest

several decision-making tricks that blend the rational and the intuitive:

1. Assess the problem's complexity

There's an argument that gut decision-making actually works best for bigger decisions, while rational methods work for smaller ones. When choosing running shoes, it's worth listing the factors involved – cost, comfort, appearance – and weighting their importance to you. But proposing marriage or changing career involves so many factors that rational analysis will make things worse: you'll fail to take account of some potential considerations, or assign too much or too little importance to others.

2. A time-honoured method for bringing unverbalised feelings into sharp focus

Take a coin, assign one option to heads, the other to tails, then toss it. But don't uncover it yet; monitor your emotions instead. What are you hoping the result will be? There's your true preference.

3. Start rational, then go intuitive

The philosopher–psychologist Paul Thagard suggests you write out your goals, your options and the likely consequences in detail. Study them. But then go with your gut. This way, you use rational methods to prepare the ground for a good intuitive judgment.

4. Set a deadline

Often, what we think of as deliberation is really hours of indecision, followed by a snap judgment. Allow yourself a period of time – a few minutes should be enough for everyday matters – to indulge this feeling. Then make that snap decision. It'll almost certainly be no worse than if you'd taken hours.

THE QUICKEST ROUTE TO BEING WRONG

It's a truism of devastating obviousness that we tend to prefer the easy option over the difficult one. Terrible choices of almost any size – from not going to the dentist for years to causing devastating oil spills – can usually be traced back to the fact that doing things differently would have taken more effort. Sure, there may be other, subtler explanations for humanity's reliable tendency towards wrongness and fiasco, but I can't be bothered to think of any. Like everyone else, I'm taking the easy option, thereby providing evidence in support of my point. Thus I win.

Even if it's a truism, though, it's only relatively recently that psychologists have come to grasp how deeply this preference for ease ferrets its way into our brains, manifesting itself not just as a liking for physical sloth, but for mental laziness, too. They call this 'cognitive fluency': the idea that if something is easy to think about, we're far more likely to think it preferable, more important or true. One study suggests that people think of recipes, or lists of tasks, as easier if they're printed in a clearer font.[86] Another suggests that hostility towards immigrants may be partially explained because it's more taxing to conceive of, say, a person from Algeria who lives in France than a French person living in France.[87] The well-known 'availability bias' makes us more afraid of threats we can vividly picture, no matter how unlikely. (The standard illustration of this, though it's hard to pin down the original statistic, is that you're 30 times more likely to be killed by a falling piece of aircraft than in a shark attack – yet who ever worries about being hit by pieces of aircraft?) An academic study of the anonymous confessions site grouphug.us concluded that people became more candid when a more legible redesign was introduced. Companies with easier-to-pronounce names, meanwhile, fare better on the stock market.[88]

This makes good evolutionary sense, of course: our brains have developed to conserve our energies for when we need them to survive. This may be why it's so hard to feel motivated to go jogging: exercise for its own sake would have been insane in a world in which you got all the workouts you needed just feeding yourself and escaping wild animals. A fondness for the familiar, similarly, is eminently understandable. As the late psychologist Robert Zajonc liked to say, 'If it's familiar, it hasn't eaten you yet.'

There's an upside to this tendency to idleness, though: cognitive fluency's opposite, 'disfluency', prompts us to think things through more carefully, and can be harnessed to prompt focused thought. Those same font researchers found that printing something in a difficult typeface caused people really to engage with the content; far more gave the correct answer to the question 'How many animals of each kind did Moses take on the ark?' (Answer: none.) The novelist Colum McCann prints off his drafts in eight-point Times New Roman, in order to peer at his words with fresh eyes and a more rigorous mind.

And yet I can't help feeling dispirited. It's agonising enough to consider the great opportunities we miss in life as a result of crippling fear, or lack of talent, or appalling bad luck. How much worse is it to think of all the roads not taken because just thinking about them in the first place took a little more effort? The only solution, presumably, is to be constantly on the alert for lazy thinking. Which is, in itself, mentally tiring. Yes. It's awkward.

GOOD NEWS FOR INTROVERTS
(JUST DON'T GO SHOUTING ABOUT IT)

According to the famous Myers–Briggs personality type test, I am an extrovert, but only very slightly. My full Myers–Briggs personality code is ENFP – a type of person described in various online sources as 'visionary', 'inspiring', 'charming', 'ingenious' and 'risk-taking'. In the decades since it was invented in the 1940s, serious scientists have queued up to demonstrate the ways in which Myers–Briggs may be so flawed as to be hopelessly inaccurate. Since receiving my results, however, I have come to the considered and unbiased conclusion that the critics are wrong. And jealous, probably. Some people, huh?

Anyway, I mention this not to brag (we ENFPs aren't boastful) but to establish that I'm not – according to Myers–Briggs, anyway – an introvert. Yet lately I've been half-wishing I were. Because, for a while now, psychologists have been re-evaluating this most maligned of personality types, and their conclusion, in short, is that being an introvert may be under-rated.

Introverts are not what the rest of us, the three-quarters of the population who are extroverts, think they are. If you're cripplingly shy and desperate to make more friends, you're probably an extrovert; if you spend time alone because you're depressed, you could be one, too. True introverts are, on balance, drained by social interaction and energised by time alone; for extroverts, the opposite applies. So you may have spent much of your life at noisy parties and not even realised you're really what Marti Laney, in her book *The Introvert Advantage*, annoyingly refers to as 'an innie'. Famous 'innies', she says, include Gwyneth Paltrow, Meryl Streep, Einstein and Al Gore, although also – just in case any introverts are tempted to start feeling superior – Enya. As a culture, Laney writes, 'we value action, speed, competition and drive. It's no wonder people are defensive about introversion'.

Introverts find social interaction tiring, according to the defenders of introversion, because they can't help but engage and empathise to a degree that extroverts habitually don't – an approach that would exhaust anybody if they did it all the time. There's a positive flipside to this, Laney argues: introverts tend to be better at sustaining long-term friendships, and to demonstrate a higher degree of sensitivity in emotional interactions. In organisations, introverts can't bring themselves to butter up people insincerely – so a boss who wants to avoid taking on yes-men and -women ought to consider hiring some introverts.

The problem is that extroverts usually can't get their minds around the idea of introversion, so they wrongly believe they're being helpful by trying to convert introverts to high-octane socialising – the 'You should get out more!' syndrome. Laney, by contrast, tells introverts they must respect their own personality type, for example by spending time alone in nature every day, rather than trying to force a fundamental character shift. Even as an extrovert, I like to think I can understand this point. But that's me: charming and ingenious, as usual.

WHAT HAPPENS IF I JUMP?

Admit it: you've felt it, too. Let's say you've climbed to the observation deck of a tall building, or tiptoed to the edge of a high cliff. Or perhaps you're on a ski-lift, dangling far above the ground. And that's when it arises – the mysterious urge that Edgar Allan Poe, who wrote about it best, calls 'a cloud of unnameable feeling'. What if you jumped? You don't want to die, of course; you're feeling generally good about life. Yet the urge is real: as Poe writes in his story *The Imp of the Perverse*, it 'chills the very marrow of our bones with the fierceness of the delight of its horror'. Acting on it would be catastrophic. But somehow it's that very fact that makes it so seductive, and so strong.

The imp is at his worst in situations involving the risk of death – is any driver immune to the idea of swerving into oncoming traffic? – but hardly confines himself to them. 'Anytime I am around a large body of water such as a river, lake or ocean, I feel tempted to throw my BlackBerry in the water,' admits one contributor to purgetheurge.com, a squirm-inducing site dedicated to the phenomenon. In hushed theatres, I sometimes have to fight the desire to yell out loud; the sheer ease with which I could ruin things for hundreds of others makes me giddy. One paper in the journal *Science* suggests these fantasies are near-universal, but also usually resisted – though we're more likely to act on them when highly stressed.[89] As Poe observes, procrastination sometimes works this way, too: 'The most important crisis of our life calls, trumpet-tongued, for immediate energy and action . . . and yet we put it off until tomorrow; and why? There is no answer, except that we feel perverse.'

This ubiquitous idiosyncrasy in our wiring seems to have little connection with suicidal thinking: the whole force of the urge comes from how much we *don't* want the results it would bring. So might it serve a purpose – could it be, in computing parlance, a feature, not a bug? Toddlers develop into autonomous, well-functioning selves by testing boundaries. Might this be the adult version of that notion? Perhaps it's useful to come face to face with what we could do if we chose, and then choose not to. (Additionally, as the philosopher David Copp points out in his book *Morality, Normativity and Society*, 'The more powerful we imagine the urge to be, the stronger the reason it gives me to back away from the edge [of the building].' Ironically, the urge may be protective.)

This is the one sense in which Poe's description of the attractions of perversity isn't true to life: his characters, plagued by the desire to commit awful acts, actually commit them. The narrator in *The Imp of the Perverse* explains how he carried out what ought to have been the perfect murder. For years afterwards, nobody suspects him, and he secretly revels in his achievement. But then, one day, a thought occurs: 'I am safe – yes – if I be not fool enough to make open confession!' Immediately, a chill creeps over him, and the urge to confess starts gnawing at his soul. He isn't suffering a crisis of conscience: the only thing driving him to reveal the truth is how disastrous it would be to do so. He does so, and is sentenced to hang. He is telling his story, he reveals, from a prison cell. The imp wins out.

HOW TO PERSUADE PEOPLE
TO DO STUPID THINGS

One finding that emerges consistently from social psychology is this: some people are just really strange. In 1966, experimenters went door to door in a suburban neighbourhood, asking residents if they'd agree to have an enormous billboard reading 'Drive Carefully' erected in their front gardens, for nothing in return. To give an idea of how it would look, they were shown a photograph of a lovely home almost completely hidden by a huge, ugly sign. Astonishingly, 17 per cent said yes.[90]

Why? No idea, and frankly they were probably beyond help to begin with. But the more interesting result concerned a subgroup of residents who'd agreed, two weeks earlier, to display a three-inch-square notice saying 'Be a Safe Driver': 76 per cent of them agreed to the billboard.

I suppose I can live with the idea that 17 per cent of people are such pushovers that they'd let a hoarding destroy their living environment just because someone with a clipboard asked them. Then again, like most people, I'd probably have agreed to the three-inch notice: I like to think I'm public-spirited. But once I'd done that, this experiment implies, it's likely I'd have said yes to the billboard, just like the oddballs. So am I an oddball, too? That's a rhetorical question; I'm not soliciting answers.

The phenomenon at work is the marketing trick known as 'incremental commitment', described by Robert Cialdini in his endlessly entertaining book *Influence*, a guide to the dark arts of 'compliance professionals' (telemarketers, charity fundraisers, prisoner-of-war camp guards – you know the type). We value consistency above almost anything and will go to extremes to maintain it. Partly, this is a matter of keeping up appearances: if you've presented yourself as committed to road safety, you may fear, albeit subconsciously, giving a contradictory impression. But it's more profound than that: once you've made a commitment, even a small one, you want to believe, deep down, that it was right. So you'll alter your actions and feelings in the direction of that conclusion. You'll genuinely want that billboard.

Another example: research suggests that after placing a bet on a horse, most people are more confident than before about its prospects.[91] What's changed is that they've invested – financially, but also psychologically, since a victory for the horse would be consistent with the decision to make the bet.

For Cialdini, this is a problem: he's worried we might act contrary to how we 'really' feel merely to seem consistent to ourselves or others. (You date someone, so you move in together, marry, have children . . . only to discover you're miserable, because you were pursuing each step to justify the last.) But the feelings that emerge in us to preserve consistency can be, he acknowledges, entirely real. And far from being a problem, that leads to a conclusion that's strangely anxiety-reducing – especially if you're fretting over some major life decision, worried about making the right choice. The consistency principle implies that whatever you choose, you're predisposed to come to feel that you chose correctly.

That massive billboard in my front garden, by the way? Best decision I ever made.

WHY ARE HORROR MOVIES FUN?

One wild and windswept afternoon – I know it should have been late at night, but it wasn't – I finally got around to watching *Paranormal Activity*, the ultra-low-budget horror film that became an underground success thanks to the curious pleasure so many people take in being scared half to death. (Don't watch it twice, then, or you may get scared fully to death.) Even at 3.30 p.m., when watched alone at home, it's an extremely creepy movie, documenting the haunting of a couple whose apartment becomes the target of a vengeful force intent on driving them to the edge of sanity with some old-school ghostly techniques: doors that suddenly slam, TVs that switch themselves on, scrapings and groanings with no discernible source. At one particularly tense point, the fridge in my kitchen started to buzz; I wheeled around, saw my own reflection in some mirrored cupboard doors and nearly yelled

out loud – which isn't, I should clarify, how I normally respond
when looking in the mirror. In short, I enjoyed myself
immensely.

But why? This mysterious truth – that so many of us seem
to find fear entertaining so long as it's fictional – has bothered
philosophers and psychologists for long enough that it has a
name: the 'horror paradox'. Encountering a chainsaw-wielding
maniac in fiction is obviously less traumatising than meeting
one at the bus stop. But why should it be actively fun? One
theory is that we simply feel a rush of relief when the horror
ends; another is that the emotion in question isn't really fear,
just excitement; a third is that we secretly love violent mayhem,
but feel able to admit it only when it's make-believe. There's
an evolutionary speculation, too: that we find blood and gore
hypnotising – the rubbernecking effect – so as to ensure that
we carefully study potential threats to our survival. But there's
little research to bolster these, and none quite captures the
thrilling blend of fear plus pleasure that a good scary film
evokes.

One more persuasive, if partial, explanation is what the
scholars Dan Ariely and Michael Norton call 'conceptual
consumption' – the idea that in a society where our most
basic needs are easily provided for, we channel our urge to
consume into the nonphysical realm: we gorge on celebrity
blogs, or seek out vicarious extreme and unfamiliar experiences, through movies and books, to add to our 'experiential
CVs', and take pleasure in the process.[92] But to explain the
fun of fear specifically, I wonder – without much evidence,
but when it comes to the horror paradox, no one has much
evidence – whether we can learn something from victims of
real horror. Survivors of accidents, armed robberies and the
like report feeling focus and clarity in the moment itself:
discursive thought, with all its associated stresses, falls away.

This is the kind of state we'd look back on, in any other circumstance, as happy absorption. Of course, once thought kicks in again, there's nothing remotely happy about their predicament. But perhaps when you're on the edge of a cinema seat, waiting to find out what's lurking behind the bedroom door, you're in a similar state of absolute, almost Zen-like focus? You are reaping the benefits of being in what seems a life-or-death situation – with the immeasurable bonus of realising, a split-second later, with delighted relief, that it isn't.

ARE YOU MORE SUPERSTITIOUS THAN YOU REALISE?

In the late 1940s, the legendary psychologist B.F. Skinner designed a series of experiments to make pigeons become superstitious. (It's surprising that the pigeon community was still prepared to work with him, because he'd spent the early part of the decade developing plans for a 'pigeon-guided missile', whereby a trained bird would be sealed inside the tip of a warhead, guiding it to its target by pecking on a screen.) During lectures, Skinner would place a pigeon in a closed box fitted with a mechanism that dispensed food pellets at fixed intervals; at the end, he'd open the lid to reveal the pigeon behaving eccentrically – pecking the floor of the box, say, or twitching in a distinctive way. It had associated the behaviour with the arrival of food, Skinner concluded: each time it repeated the peck or the twitch, another pellet eventually appeared, reinforcing the link.[93] Human super-stitions draw on the same idea. Hold your breath when an ambulance passes and you will indeed find, in almost every case, that you don't die shortly afterwards. Avoid saying

'Macbeth' backstage at a play, and behold: the theatre probably won't burn down.

Naturally, those of us who consider ourselves intelligent and sober-minded (you too, huh?) scoff at such irrational beliefs. But we probably shouldn't: in subtler forms, superstition infects us all, argues Marshall Goldsmith, an 'executive coach' hired to advise the heads of firms such as Ford, Toyota and GlaxoSmithKline. 'In many cases,' he notes, 'the higher we climb the organisational totem pole, the more superstitious we become.'

Goldsmith's point isn't that the chief executive of Ford tries not to step on cracks when he walks down the street. The damaging role that superstition played in the lives of Goldsmith's clients was in their beliefs about how they'd achieved their status. 'One of the greatest mistakes of successful people,' he writes in his book *What Got You Here Won't Get You There*, 'is the assumption, "I am successful. I behave this way. Therefore, I must be successful because I behave this way!"' They don't see that their behaviour may be irrelevant, as with the pigeons – or, worse, that they may have succeeded in spite of it. For example: 'I've worked with executives who insist their remoteness, inscrutable silences [and] non-accessibility [are a] calculated tactic to get people to think for themselves.' Stubbornly pursuing what you think caused your success, he warns, can lead you to sabotage it.

Stress sometimes works this way, too. We take on a challenge, worry about it, succeed, then subconsciously associate the worry with the success, initiating a vicious circle that ends in burnout. It's not just a workplace matter, either: as Goldsmith notes, the same false linkages can blight how we approach personal relationships. 'You might be shocked at how superstitious you really are,' he concludes. Your brain works much like a pigeon's. Sorry about that.

THE LIMITS OF WILLPOWER

As a rule, it's important not to confuse serious psychiatric disorders with the normal ups and downs of life. Just because you're feeling low, it doesn't mean you're 'depressed'; just because you're easily distracted, it doesn't mean you've got attention deficit disorder. But I'm going to have to make an exception in the case of 'utilisation behaviour', a medical phenomenon I happened upon recently with a shock of recognition. It afflicts people who have suffered severe damage to the frontal lobes of their brains . . . and me. And probably you, too.

Patients displaying utilisation behaviour can't stop themselves automatically using whatever things enter their visual field: they can't pass a door without opening it, a telephone without picking it up, a light switch without flicking it.

Remind you of anyone? I'm not actually suggesting that you can't resist opening doors, but it's scary to consider how much our lives are determined not by conscious decisions but by whatever happens to present itself: food that gets eaten because it's there; evenings spent watching TV because there's a TV in the room. Or bigger things: a job you fell into because it came along, or a relationship. (Headline from *The Onion*: '18-year-old Miraculously Finds Soulmate in Hometown'.) It's been argued that utilisation behaviour might account for a lot of what we call absent-mindedness, too: we're accustomed to putting things back in the fridge, say, so when we walk past the fridge, we open it and deposit whatever we're carrying, even if it's the car keys.

Resisting the power of our surroundings takes effort. In one fascinating study, a team of psychologists including Roy

Baumeister, a pioneer in research on self-control, asked people to complete tasks that required 'effortful persistence' and focus – the equivalent of such real-world challenges as remaining at your desk to work instead of wandering off to make another coffee, or walking past a shop window without making an impulse purchase. The tasks, it turned out, depleted their glucose levels; moreover, subjects who had a glucose drink beforehand showed more persistence. Exerting self-control, in other words, uses up real energy, much as lifting a heavy object does.[94] Another surprising moral would seem to be: drink a sugary drink before starting work.

Baumeister calls this effect 'ego depletion', because we're imposing our sense of self on the world, and on our behaviour, and the effort involved is a limited resource. We use it up. This is why experimental subjects who are asked to prevent themselves from laughing while watching a funny video perform less well at subsequent tasks that require focus: they have temporarily used up their willpower reserves.[95] It's also why, if you want to change some behaviour, willpower can be only a temporary or partial solution. It's exhaustible, and if you rely on it too much in one area – eating healthily, say – you may find that you don't have enough left over for the rest of life. (Instead of relying on willpower, we need to develop routines, so that things become automatic.) There'll be lots of healthy food in your fridge, but you'll probably keep leaving your car keys in there, too.

WHY YOU SHOULDN'T RESIST TEMPTATION

A few years ago, Citibank launched an advertising campaign entitled 'Live richly', making the case that actively enjoying your life was more important than obsessively stewarding your savings and investments. This enraged me for multiple reasons – above all, I *want* my bank to be boringly obsessed with my money, not dispensing self-help advice – and Citibank's subsequent fortunes suggest that a little more obsessive stewarding might not have gone amiss. (Its new slogan, in the United States, is 'Citi never sleeps': I see what they're getting at, but it makes me think of terrified, insomniac bankers, which isn't much of an improvement.) Still, it's worth asking if the message – despite the messenger – might not contain wisdom. Assailed daily by anxiety-inducing economic news, are we in danger of becoming too careful with money?

This sounds like ostentatious contrarianism. We rarely think of ourselves as spending too little and saving too much. Decades of psychological research testify to the curse of myopia – our tendency to take a short-term, impulsive approach to money, splurging in haste and repenting at leisure. But we can also fall victim to myopia's opposite, hyperopia – an excessive far-sightedness that leaves us pining for the pleasure we might have had.

The passage of time does strange things to our feelings about virtue and vice. Shortly after splashing out on an indulgence, we may feel buyer's remorse, but that usually fades quickly. The regret we feel about denying ourselves an indulgence, by contrast, starts small and grows bigger. When the American researchers Ran Kivetz and Anat Keinan asked students what they regretted about a recent college holiday, they said they wished they'd studied harder, or worked to earn money. But students asked about a holiday that happened a year ago were more likely to regret not travelling and having more fun. For attendees at a fortieth-anniversary college reunion, looking back on their student days, that regret was even more acute.[96] As the researchers put it, 'Choices of virtue over vice evoke increasing regret': the 'wistful feeling of missing out on the pleasures of life' grows worse as the period in question vanishes into one's past. This isn't just a matter of regretting the things we don't do more than the things we do (though that's true), since partying and studying both involve taking actions. It's just that the guilt of succumbing to temptation soon dissipates, while the sense of missing out does not.

Intuitively, people understand hyperopia's risks. In another of Kivetz's studies, a third of women entering a lottery chose the chance to win an $80 spa voucher, rather than $85 in cash. Apparently, they were 'precommitting' themselves to pleasure: they knew that if they took the cash, they'd put it in the bank or spend it too sensibly.[97]

The irony is that we feel guiltiest about what we enjoy the most – so we may be more likely to deny ourselves the luxuries we love than those we feel less strongly about. Kivetz and Keinan quote the author James Branch Cabell, offering a useful dissenting thought for today's edgy recessionary era: 'There is no memory with less satisfaction than the memory of some temptation we resisted.'

CHAPTER 7

HOW TO KEEP
FUNCTIONING

Everyday Life

IS IT JUST ME, OR IS
MODERN LIFE ACTUALLY OK?

There are few aspects of modern life more irritating than people who go on and on about the aspects of modern life they find really irritating. Is the over-loud use of mobile phones on trains, for example, genuinely more annoying than the very existence of the BBC TV series *Grumpy Old Men*, where the phenomenon is moaned about incessantly? Is walking into a greengrocer's and seeing a misplaced apostrophe really worse than walking into a bookshop and not being able to breathe for copies of *Eats, Shoots and Leaves*? And what about the book *Is It Just Me or Is Everything Shit*? ('Or is it just this book?', as the writer Bill Bryson once superbly put it in a newspaper interview.) And, yes, I realise this paragraph constitutes precisely the sort of list of annoyances that I'm professing to hate. I irritate myself all the time, believe me.

There's a kernel of useful truth in all this whining, however, which is this: it really is the tiny things that seem to provoke the most anger. Psychologists call these 'background stressors', the small but unremitting factors that build up and may even trigger or exacerbate illness – or shooting sprees in Midwestern shopping malls, for that matter – as surely as bigger and more obviously traumatic experiences.[98] The fact that they're so small, of course, doubles their power of irritation: you get to be infuriated by your upstairs neighbour's creaky floorboard and, additionally, infuriated that you're getting infuriated by something so minor.

A lot of this we simply have to tolerate. (In your working life, it has been demonstrated, you'll suffer from background stressors in proportion to how little control you have over your environment, which is why waiters and drivers experience their ill-effects infinitely more than, say, the well-off talking heads on *Grumpy Old Men*.[99]) But we can change some things. One obvious but fantastically useful exercise is as follows: take a sheet of paper and a pen. Walk through your home or workplace, making a note of the physical things that cause you a few seconds' annoyance on a daily basis (a loose door-handle; not having enough socks; the bag of clothes you've been meaning to take to the charity shop for months). Choose the most annoying one. Fix it now. That's the end of the exercise. The investment, in terms of time, is tiny; the payoff, in terms of serenity, is huge.

Of course, a good Buddhist would chime in here and observe that true serenity is about remaining calm in the midst of daily irritations, not trying to control your surroundings to the point where the irritations don't exist. 'It doesn't matter what you're given, [whether] it's life in a madhouse or life in the middle of a peaceful, silent desert,' writes the American Buddhist nun Pema Chödrön. 'Whatever you're given can wake you up or put you to sleep.' The way to think about the idiot on the train who's talking too loudly on his mobile phone, from this perspective, is that he's generously providing you with an opportunity to learn to become less irritable. Well, it's something to aim for.

THE CONTRADICTIONS OF COMMUTING

The United States Census periodically issues reports on a category of workers it labels 'extreme commuters', which brings to mind images of eccentric Americans paragliding to the office, but which really means, less thrillingly, that they spend three hours or more travelling between work and home.

(Presumably there are a few who paraglide to the office, though; one imagines they live on the west coast, work at Google and use the word 'dude' a lot.) Extreme commuting is on the rise, and not just in the US: one survey not long ago found 10 per cent of Britons spending two or more hours a day on the road.[100] This is one of commuting's vicious ironies: if you live somewhere big and spread-out, it'll take you ages to get to work; but if you live somewhere small and crowded, it'll take you ages, too, albeit for different reasons.

Another irony: people commute reluctantly, when they have no choice, because they can't afford to live closer to work – yet if they get rich, they're liable to do it to an even greater degree, presumably because they think living in the countryside, or quasi-countryside, will make them happier. The former kind of commuter won't be remotely surprised to learn that it often doesn't: numerous studies have shown commuting to be among the most misery-inducing of daily activities, highly correlated with stress and social isolation, often far outweighing the benefits.[101]

The Swiss economists Alois Stutzer and Bruno Frey call this the 'commuter's paradox', though really it's less of a paradox than a cognitive mistake: people chronically underestimate the downsides of a long commute, while overestimating the upsides of (say) a bigger house. The average one-hour-each-way commuter, they concluded, would need 40 per cent more pay to declare him or herself as 'satisfied' as a non-commuter.[102] The neuroscience writer Jonah Lehrer suggests that this may be partly because commuting, especially in car traffic, is unpredictable, so we never get used to it. The brain's capacity for adapting to the predictable usually seems like a disadvantage: it explains the 'hedonic treadmill', whereby the thrill of a new car, or some other longed-for benefit, soon fades. But it also means that if you must have aggravations, it's best if they're as regular as clockwork. We imagine a long commute will be a slightly tiresome ritual. Instead, it's a fresh challenge every day.

Non-commuters needn't feel smug, though, because freely chosen long commutes are surely an example of a thinking error we all make in other contexts. You might call it the 'best of both worlds' fallacy: faced with opposing choices, we struggle to combine the benefits of each, yet ignore the costs – in time, money and energy – of doing the combining. Commuters do this, but so does your annoying friend who tries to pack three social events into a single evening, spending almost no time at each, and leaving everyone involved mildly irritated. Even the serene-sounding notion of a 'balanced life', which we're always being exhorted to attain, often seems to compound the problem: if the very act of balancing work, family, friends, hobbies, relaxation and travel wears you out, perhaps an unbalanced life isn't such a bad idea after all.

Of course, there are those who seem to relish commuting – to appreciate the quiet isolation of the car or the iPod buds, or the sense of transition between work and non-work. But there are people who like death metal, too, and Cherry Coke. It's an odd world.

WHY IS SUNDAY THE MOST
DEPRESSING DAY OF THE WEEK?

You probably didn't need researchers at the University of Gothenburg in Sweden to tell you that Sunday is the most depressing day of the week. Few emotions are as instantly familiar as that deflating, edgy-yet-lethargic feeling seared into our psyches in childhood, and in Britain often accompanied by memories of bygone BBC programming, usually classic adaptations of Charles Dickens novels. Still, to rub it in, the Swedes analysed interviews with thousands of people – Germans, as it happens – so the folk wisdom about Sundays is now, in the language of media headlines, 'official'. There were nuances: married people experienced the Sunday mood-plunge more than the unmarried, and former west Germans felt it more than former east Germans (though they were gloomier to start with). But, overall, Sundays were saddest.[103] And they don't show many BBC classic serials in Germany, so that can't be the reason.

At first glance, the real explanation seems unmysterious: it's the day before work or school restarts. These are the last hours of freedom, suffused with anticipation of unwilling toil. But there's more to it than that: the modern Sunday, I think, is a lesson in how not to structure your life – or society – for maximum happiness.

The first hint that Sunday gloom isn't simply a rational response to returning to work comes from remembering what happens when we actually get to work: many of us, as has frequently been observed, tend to enjoy the structure and goal-focus of our jobs. (In his book *The Labour of Leisure*, for example, the sociologist Chris Rojek argues that free time takes as much effort as 'unfree' work.) But Sunday carries more meaning than 'the day before work': it's meant to be (historically) an especially spiritually edifying day, or (nowadays) an especially relaxing, convivial one. And so it ignores two key rules of happiness. First, as soon as you label any period as 'specially' enjoyable, you'll become so self-conscious, monitoring its specialness, that enjoyment is near-impossible. And second, in a culture that's no longer mono-religious, being told which day to set aside triggers an inevitable rebelliousness. I rarely want to go supermarket shopping on a Sunday evening until I remember that in Britain it's essentially forbidden. Add to all this Sunday's role as a temporal punctuation mark – 'Reading the papers, drinking tea, ironing, a few more hours, and another week gone,' as Jimmy Porter puts it in *Look Back in Anger* – and it's a bust. You couldn't invent a more dispiriting day if you tried.

Which explains why campaigns to 'keep Sunday special' seem doomed, on their own terms, and leaving aside their Christian bias: you can't impose specialness. Perhaps we need strong laws to protect shopworkers' hours, but that's a separate matter. Meanwhile, stopping people doing what they want on Sunday won't automatically prompt them to do something more enjoyable, let alone more worthwhile. The United Kingdom's 'Keep Sunday Special' campaign doesn't even have the courage of its convictions: it lobbies to protect the current compromise of limited Sunday trading hours, which creates neither a shopping-free nor a frustration-free day.

Back in Germany, responding to a complaint from the churches, a court declared that relaxing Sunday trading laws would be unconstitutional on the grounds that Sundays should be for 'spiritual elevation'. Maybe they should; I'm no free-market extremist or hardcore atheist. But court-ordered spiritual elevation? Good luck with that.

WHY BAD HABITS ARE SO HARD TO BREAK

Everyone knows that it takes 28 days to develop a new habit, or perhaps 21, or 18, depending on who you ask; anyway, the point is that it's a specific number, which makes it sound scientific and thus indisputably true. We probably owe this particular example of pop-psychology wisdom to Maxwell Maltz, the plastic surgeon who wrote the 1960s bestseller *Psycho-Cybernetics*. He claimed to have observed that amputees took an average of only 21 days to adjust to the loss of a limb. Therefore, he reasoned – deploying the copper-bottomed logic we've come to expect from self-help – the same must be true of all big changes. And therefore it must take 21 days to change a habit, maybe, perhaps!

This is, of course, poppycock and horsefeathers, as a new study by the University College London psychologist Phillippa Lally and her colleagues helps confirm.[104] On average, her subjects, who were trying to learn new habits such as eating fruit daily or going jogging, took a depressing 66 days before reporting that the behaviour had become unchangingly automatic. Individuals ranged widely – some took 18 days, others 245 – and some habits, unsurprisingly, were harder than others to make stick: one especially silly implication of the 28- or 21-day rule is that it may be just as easy to start eating a few more apples as to start finding five hours a week to study Chinese. (Another myth undermined by the study is the idea that when forming a new habit, you can't miss a day or all is lost: missing a day made no difference. Indeed, believing this myth may be actively unhelpful, making it harder to restart once you fall off the wagon.)

Self-help culture clings to the fiction of the 28-day rule, presumably, because it makes habit-change sound plausibly difficult enough, but basically easy. The first problem with this is dispiritingly simple: changing habits is hard. We're all 'cognitive misers', our brains designed to take short cuts, rendering as many behaviours as possible automatic. 'Really,' asks the psychologist Ian Newby-Clark, on the website of *Psychology Today*, 'what would be the point of having a habit that didn't free up your mind to crunch on more pressing matters?' Habits are meant to be difficult to change.

The subtler problem is that we tend to think about habit-change wrongly. (I'm not talking about physiological addictions

here, which need a different kind of approach.) We get trapped
in a paradox: we want to, say, stop watching so much TV, but
on the other hand, demonstrably, we also want to watch lots
of TV – after all, we keep doing it – so what we really want,
it seems, is to stop wanting. We're mired deep in what the
Greeks called '*akrasia*': deciding on the best course of action,
then doing something else. The way round this, say Newby-
Clark and others, is to see that habits are responses to needs.
This sounds obvious, but countless efforts at habit-change
ignore its implications. If you eat badly, you might resolve to
start eating well, but if you're eating burgers and ice-cream
to feel comforted, relaxed and happy, trying to replace them
with broccoli and carrot juice is like dealing with a leaky
bathroom tap by repainting the kitchen. What's required isn't
a better diet, but an alternative way to feel comforted and
relaxed. 'The chains of habit are too weak to be felt until they
are too strong to be broken,' Dr Johnson observed gloomily,
but maybe by looking at the problem differently we can still,
Houdini-like, slip out of them.

STOP COMPLAINING!

The Reverend Will Bowen is the pastor of Christ Church
Unity in Kansas City, Missouri. It's conceivable that not
everybody reading this will leap to take advice from a Christian
minister in a conservative American state. It probably doesn't
help, either, that Bowen has written a book, and launched a
global phenomenon, challenging people to stop complaining
for 21 days straight. The title, *A Complaint-Free World*, smacks
of self-help's conformist bias: who wants to be a compliant
cog in the machine anyhow? Besides, perhaps you enjoy
complaining. I like few things better than firing off witheringly

pompous letters to utilities companies who treat me with contempt and incompetence. I understand that this may strike you as pitiful.

'I'm not a good little cog,' Bowen told me before I tried his challenge, which involves wearing a purple plastic wristband and switching it from wrist to wrist when you catch yourself complaining. 'I learned this British term: whingeing. Dissatisfaction is the first step to positive change. But I'm saying take more control, make the change you want; don't just whinge.'

What began as a local project has mushroomed, and now millions of purple bracelets have been distributed through complaintfreeworld.org. Out of self-consciousness, I switched mine from pocket to pocket, not wrist to wrist, but as Bowen readily accepts, you don't really need one at all – you can use any small object. This is a venerable behavioural therapy trick for inculcating any new habit.

Complaining, Bowen says, doesn't include neutrally telling someone they're doing something wrong, let alone speaking up against abusive treatment; he's talking, specifically, about the kind of moaning that just makes us feel worse – and which we vent, mostly, on friends who can't do anything about it, rather than the person or institution we want to change. On average, Bowen says, it takes five to seven months for people to reach twenty-one complaint-free days; I haven't made it past two. And, as the process made horribly clear, I don't spend much of my life getting righteously angry about economic injustice or warfare: I spend it whingeing about people, or about tasks that end up taking less time than the whingeing. And, unscientifically, I'd say I felt far better when I wasn't whingeing. Talking about problems is often important, but sometimes, not talking helps.

Bowen ropes in an old joke to illustrate his point that we

complain not to change things but as an alternative to doing so. Two builders eat their packed lunches together. Day after day, one finds he's got meatloaf sandwiches and complains – 'Another meatloaf sandwich?' – until finally his colleague can't contain himself. 'Why don't you just ask your wife to make you something else?' he suggests. 'What are you talking about?' his friend says. 'I make my own lunch.'

FRUGALITY FOR FUN AND PROFIT

Reading an excessive number of self-help books inevitably causes one to internalise some of their outlook on life, and this has been causing me difficulties with regard to the current economic crisis. I haven't reached the stage of screaming, 'You're poor because you chose to be poor!' at homeless people. (I refer you to the obnoxious Larry Winget, author of *You're Broke Because You Want to Be* – although Winget's obnoxiousness is a pose, and, to be fair, he's only making explicit an attitude that's implicit in many other books: if you're not super-rich, you're not trying hard enough.) On the other hand, I've evidently absorbed enough positive thinking to find myself growing impatient during conversations in which friends – usually friends who aren't at imminent risk of penury – try to outdo each other with gloomy predictions. It's not that the economic situation isn't extremely serious. It's just that all this competitive upsetting doesn't seem, particularly, to help.

So I've been delighted to discover a handful of blogs dedicated to the topic of frugality that take things seriously yet not fatalistically, thereby managing – against all odds – to make the process of not spending money actively enjoyable. (I'm aware that frugal behaviour may make matters worse, on a macroeconomic scale, but if you're reading this book for macroeconomic wisdom, God help you.) The best of these sites, including thesimpledollar.com and getrichslowly.org, apply the phenomenon of 'lifehacking' – simple tricks for happier and more productive living – to money management, thereby transforming it from a chore to a geeky project, which people like me find fun.

The frugality-hackers' key insight is that, while everyone knows humans are irrational about money, most personal finance advice assumes we're rational. Tried keeping to a personal budget recently? As with any solution dependent on self-discipline, the constant vigilance is exhausting. Instead, argues Trent Hamm of The Simple Dollar, you have to find ways to make it more convenient not to spend money than to spend it, which might involve something as basic as leaving your credit card at home. Of course, if you can possibly afford it, you should be spiriting a portion of your pay-cheque into a hard-to-access account. Most of us live up to our means; tricking your brain into believing your means are smaller than they are is the least painful way to save.

Or take debt. If you have multiple debts, conventional wisdom dictates paying off the one with the highest interest rate, where possible; otherwise, you're bleeding money. But lifehackers prefer the 'debt snowball': regardless of interest rates, start with the smallest balance, then the next, etcetera. It doesn't make mathematical sense. But the psychological boost that comes from quickly eliminating a debt, then another, will provide momentum to keep going. Everyone's irrational, to some degree. The challenge is to work with your irrationality, not against it.

Should you need further evidence that we're not logical about money, by the way, consider the American study in which people responded much more favourably to an

offer of receiving 300 cents than 3 dollars.[105] Sometimes,
one despairs.

THE STRANGE PSYCHOLOGY OF QUEUEING

In the 1980s, the psychologist Stanley Milgram sent 130
researchers into New York with a simple mission: queue-
jumping. Milgram is better known for his studies on obedience,
in which ordinary people were induced to give dangerous
electric shocks – or so they believed – to unseen victims.
Perhaps his queue-jumping experiment wasn't so controversial,
but it was provocative enough: researchers were told to find
a queue, enter it between the third and fourth person with
the words, 'Excuse me, I'd like to get in here', and see what
happened. What happened was this: half the time, no one said
a thing; only 10 per cent of the time was there a serious
confrontation.[106] Milgram speculated that this wasn't just
because people fear conflict, but because every member of a
queue has an interest in keeping it orderly: better to absorb
a solitary rulebreaker in silence than to lose your place to
admonish the culprit, or risk a fight that slows everyone down
or triggers the collapse of the queue. Respect for this firm-
but-flexible orderliness must be why the British love queues,
since it surely can't be that we're a nation of sheep who enjoy
delays because they give us something to moan about.

Queues aren't just a microcosm of the unspoken rules
governing human interaction. For many of us, they're also the
context in which we most often confront impatience and
frustration, those ubiquitous, low-level obstacles to a happy
life. Companies know this, and deploy numerous tactics to
make the time pass more quickly. Indefinite waits seem longer
than defined ones, writes the business guru David Maister in

his paper 'The Psychology of Waiting Lines', which is why Disney theme parks use complex formulae to calculate and display wait-times.[107] 'Pre-process' waits seem longer than 'in-process' waits, which is why restaurants will seat you before they're ready to serve you. Customers are happier when queues are acknowledged: when a supermarket calls 'all staff to the checkouts', it's as much about you hearing it as about staffing. And occupied time passes faster than unoccupied time: mirrored walls are especially effective, apparently because most people love looking at themselves.

If you're in the mood for self-improvement, queues are also the perfect opportunity to develop what the psychotherapist Albert Ellis called 'high frustration tolerance' – observing our thoughts and learning to distinguish preferences ('I'd like to get served soon') from the absolutist 'musts' that cause negative emotions ('I must get served soon, and this waiting is intolerable!'). And queues bring sharply into focus how much of our lives we spend in a queue-like state of mind, leaning into the future, absorbed in thoughts about later, wanting it not to be now. Can you, as Eckhart Tolle suggests, relax into the waiting instead, treating it as an oasis, a pause in the rush of events?

Yeah, me, neither. But it's worth a try: figure out how to find enjoyment in a queue, and you'll be able to find it in almost anything.

NEWS YOU CAN LOSE

I'm surprised how frequently I encounter the idea – from writers on happiness, but also sometimes from friends – that a good way to improve your life is to stop consuming news. (CNN, some of these people like to joke, stands for 'Constant

Negative News'.) As a news junkie, I've always bridled at this: don't we have a moral obligation to know what's going on in the world? I realise this may seem self-interested, since I spend much of my life writing articles for newspapers, but that's not the case. Or, more precisely, it is the case – but it's one of those occasions when my morals align with my self-interest. In short: if you ever encounter a newspaper in which I have written an article, it's your duty, as an educated citizen of a democracy, to buy a copy. Several, actually.

Still, the arguments of the no-news advocates aren't unconvincing. 'The only reason for making news daily,' claims John Somerville in *How the News Makes Us Dumb*, 'is to create an information industry': news organisations have a vested interest in encouraging a sense of the world as 'jumpy and scattered', as he puts it, and constantly changing. News is biased: not primarily politically, though that's sometimes true, but in favour of crises, which combine novelty with negativity. And for what? Few of us respond by travelling to help suffering people, and most of the time we don't even give money. Instead, we just feel worse. (There are 'good news' websites to counteract this, but I can't take them seriously: 'Milkman Still Delivering' was the lead headline when I visited happynews.com, above a story about a jovial gent resisting the decline of his trade.)

Nor is feeling bad the only effect. The maverick economist Nassim Taleb once told me (in an interview for a newspaper, no less) that he shuns newspapers in the belief that they actively make you stupid. Each day they must generate fresh stories, so what an engineer would call their 'signal to noise' ratio is poor: you have to wait weeks, even years, to see which of the events they presented as significant really turned out to be so.

What finally tipped me into trying a news-fast was the suggestion, made by the evolutionary psychologist Deirdre

Barrett, that news might be a 'supernormal stimulus'. Since we've evolved to respond to certain stimuli, this theory goes, artificial versions of those stimuli can trick us. Some songbirds, she explains, prefer to sit on lurid, oversized, fake versions of their real eggs. An obvious human parallel is pornography, which exploits a sort of evolutionary deception, since being attracted to pictures of bodies – as opposed to real ones – clearly isn't a great way to replicate your genes. What if news works like this too? In prehistoric times, it made sense to be hungry for information that might affect our survival, and fascinated by new events that might signal danger or opportunity. But 'combing the planet for the largest, most dramatic disasters,' Barrett writes in her book *Supernormal Stimuli*, exploits that hunger while bringing us little advantage.

And so I tried. Only for six days (for professional reasons). Over the first two days, the phrase 'news junkie' took on new meaning. I felt like recovering addicts must. I watched my hand creep to the mouse button or the radio on-switch, and didn't always intercept it in time. Then things got noticeably more peaceful. I met a friend in a bar; he mentioned a news story I hadn't heard, but it didn't impede our conversation. Later, a long magazine profile that I wanted to read presented a dilemma: was it news? I decided to be strict, and deem that it was.

Like I say, this didn't last. I continue to think basic familiarity with the news is important. But as with many exercises in renunciation, the real benefit wasn't in eradicating something from my life; it was in becoming more conscious of what I let in. I still want to know there's been an earthquake in the Pacific or a new financial crisis in the Eurozone. I may even want to know the details. But I want to make that decision, not have my instincts make it for me. And I almost certainly don't need to know that Lindsay Lohan has been released from jail, or that Russell Crowe has thrown a telephone at someone. 'There are many things of which a wise man might wish to be ignorant,' observed Ralph Waldo Emerson. Which is, as it happens, exactly my attitude towards the vast majority of Lohan- and Crowe-related developments.

THE IRONIES OF INSOMNIA

The last thing anybody who suffers from insomnia needed to hear was the finding, from sleep scientists at the universities of Warwick and Naples, that consistently getting fewer than six hours' sleep a night may lead to an early death.[108] Well, thanks a bunch: what news could be more likely to induce sleeplessness? Now, instead of just spending the small, silent hours contemplating death in the manner of Philip Larkin ('Waking at four to soundless dark, I stare'), insomniacs get to chew over the possibility that their very wakefulness might be hastening the death they're contemplating. How ironically hilarious! Apart from the bit where you die.

As the persistently sleep-deprived won't need telling, such ironies run deep in insomnia, which is victim to what the Harvard psychologist Daniel Wegner calls 'ironic processes of mental control': trying to get to sleep is a sure-fire way to fail. And this is only one example: efforts to suppress negative thoughts or to eliminate anxiety are all prone, Wegner argues, to the same devilish mechanism. You try to control your own mind in some way, but can't help triggering an internal monitoring process that watches to see if you're succeeding – and that disrupts the whole business. You grow hyper-alert about not being asleep, anxious about your anxiety, upset about failing to think happy thoughts. (The classic experiment involves asking participants not to think of a white bear. Try it for 60 seconds, starting . . . now. Failed already, right?) Trying deliberately to stay awake seems a possible solution, and can work for a while, but then you remember you're doing it only to achieve its opposite, whereupon self-monitoring kicks back in and all is lost.

Should we even be trying, though? As a rather mild sufferer, I'm on thin ice suggesting to hardcore insomniacs that there might be something in their condition worth not hating, or at least getting curious about. But don't take it from me: take it from the Romanian philosopher-insomniac E.M. Cioran, who saw in sleeplessness something essentially human. 'The importance of insomnia is so colossal that I am tempted to define man as the animal who cannot sleep,' he once wrote. There is 'not another animal in the entire creation that wants to sleep yet cannot'.

During those sleepless night stretches, when for most insomniacs everyday worries take on giant proportions right when we can do least about them, Cioran felt himself to be encountering truth, existence in the raw, even the meaning of life. 'He ultimately understood his long journeys into the sickly morning light as both crushing him and yet shaping his sensibilities,' observes the Cioran scholar Gordon Marino in a *New York Times* essay. 'What rich or strange idea,' Cioran asks, 'was ever the work of a sleeper?' In those weird hours, out of sync with the rest of the world, his singular creativity flourished. The experience wasn't much fun, but it was real.

Perhaps that's extreme: almost nobody these days is best advised to get less sleep. But at least Cioran reminds us that special atmospheres attach to those parts of the 24-hour cycle decoupled from the world's routine. Getting up at 4 a.m. can feel magical, if it's voluntary; medieval peasants often slept in two phases, 'first sleep' and 'second sleep', with a much-valued

period of peaceful half-wakefulness between. Being awake at
night has its upsides. Though if you truly come to believe
that, you'll probably find you can't do it.

ARE YOUR POSSESSIONS OUT TO GET YOU?

'The goal of all inanimate objects,' the author Russell Baker
famously once declared, 'is to resist man and ultimately defeat
him.' This philosophy – first aired in *The Spectator* in 1948,
where it was labelled 'resistentialism' – is described by
Wikipedia as a 'jocular theory'. Well, perhaps. But one rarely
feels jocular when confronted by it. For example, I defy anyone
to use a Nokia 6500 phone handset (yes, that's the one that
sometimes takes a photograph while you're sending a text
message, thereby deleting the message – welcome to my life)
and remain jocular for long. Besides, the conspiracy of objects
is well organised. If the Nokia doesn't get you, one of its
associates will: the toe-stubbing floorboard, the self-assembly
bookshelf, the unopenable jar.

Of course, our emotional relationships with objects aren't
characterised solely by paranoia. They're as varied as our
feelings about people. What I feel for my bathroom shower
is a sort of low-level contempt: it's a slacker; it doesn't put in
sufficient effort. What I feel for my Moleskine hardback
notebooks, meanwhile, is genuine warmth. Such emotions, if
not usually very intense, are pervasive: you almost certainly
spend more time, overall, in the company of your mobile
phone than your spouse, children or friends, and how you
feel about it will surely impact on your happiness. 'The
principles for designing pleasurable, effective interaction
between people and products,' writes the designer Donald
Norman in his superb book *Emotional Design*, 'are the very

same ones that support pleasurable and effective interaction between individuals.'

Marketers love to blather about the importance of emotion, but they're talking about what Norman calls the 'reflective' level of design – the brand you're buying into when you purchase, say, an iPod, and what that says about you. Norman's focus is on the 'visceral' level, which is deeply physical, sensual, and probably entrenched in us thanks to evolution. A solid, well-built, well-proportioned table just feels right, regardless of what statement you're making by owning it. More complex electronic devices, by contrast, seem reserved and inscrutable, shielding their inner workings from view. 'One side-effect of today's technologically advanced world,' Norman notes, 'is that it is not uncommon to hate the things we interact with.'

These are all just dumb objects, a rationalist might protest. Why get invested? But we do, and, as Norman explains, this instinctive anthropomorphising is not that odd. After all, we attribute intentional behaviour to a phone or a shower by inferring its attitude towards us from its outward behaviour – which is, ultimately, all we can do with humans, too. Think of the person you're closest to in the world: how weird is it to realise that, in fact, you've never known anything about the content of his or her mind, except what you've inferred from their movements and the sounds they make with their vocal cords?

If we can't fight this anthropomorphising, we might as well nurture it wisely, and make sure we're surrounded, as far as possible, by objects that make us happy. Perhaps that sounds indulgent – but friendly and attractive objects needn't be expensive ones. In fact, in my experience, expensive things are more likely to have a bad attitude. They act as if they're entitled. My lazy shower wasn't cheap; it just can't be bothered. One of these days, it's going to find itself getting replaced.

THREE SHORTCUTS TO
MAKING BETTER DECISIONS

I feel slightly sorry for Suzy Welch, the self-help guru behind the book *10–10–10: A Life-Transforming Idea*. Welch's '10–10–10' method for taking decisions is genuinely wise. When faced with any dilemma, she advises, ask yourself: what will the consequences be in ten minutes, ten months and ten years? This process 'surfaces our unconscious agendas', Welch claims, though what it most obviously does is properly balance short- and long-term perspectives, avoiding both hedonistic impulsiveness and a grim-faced fixation with the future. 'Sound simple? Not quite,' warns the book's publicity material. Actually, though, it is simple. That's its strength – but it also means that, unsportingly, I've now told you everything important in the book. That I can do this so briefly is surely, sales-wise, a problem.

Yet decision-making tricks such as 10-10-10 ought to be ridiculously simple, because we need them most when it comes to addressing the countless minor dilemmas that crowd our days. Momentous life-choices, by contrast, can be dwelt on and discussed with friends. But it's a curious fact that many people seem to find the insignificant choices at least as paralysing as the big ones – a truth I've had many opportunities to ponder while waiting for my father, not an indecisive man on the macro-level, to agonise over toppings in pizza restaurants. Here are three more shortcuts for taking everyday decisions:

1. 5–3–1

A dependable tactic for two people choosing a restaurant or movie: one person picks five options, the other narrows the field to three, then the first person selects one. This 'has saved me and my girlfriend from starving to death on more than one occasion', writes one grateful commenter at Ask Metafilter (ask.metafilter.com). (Hint: couples should agree in advance to use this rule, so that 'whether or not to use 5–3–1' doesn't become a dilemma itself.)

2. Be a satisficer, not a maximiser

'Satisficing', coined by the economist Herbert Simon, essentially means not letting the best be the enemy of the good, but it's more rigorous than that. Rather than trying to pick the best bed-and-breakfast, for example, decide first on the criteria that matter most – 'near woodland', 'serves a great breakfast' and 'in Wales', perhaps – then select the very first one you encounter that ticks all the boxes. This is far less exhausting, and may actually bring you closer to the 'best', by focusing your mind on what matters, rather than on alluring advertising or other distractions.

3. The 37 per cent rule

This is for sequential choices, where each option must be accepted or rejected in turn – as in flat-hunting, where an option may vanish if you hesitate, or, say, choosing where to picnic while hiking (assuming you don't want to retrace your steps). Provided you can estimate the total number of options – the number of flats you're prepared to look at, the number of potential picnic spots – it's a weird mathematical truth that your best bet is to reject the first 37 per cent of them, then pick the first one that's better than any of those first 37 per cent. (If none is, pick the final one instead.) According to an article in *Lecture Notes in Economics and Mathematical Systems*, this can be applied to choosing a mate, too.[109] But maybe that publication's not the greatest place to look for romantic advice.

ZEN AND THE ART OF TRAVELLING LIGHT

One day, perhaps when it comes up in a pub quiz, or a
particularly obscure edition of Trivial Pursuit, you'll thank me
for sharing the following piece of information: the legendary
disc jockey and eccentric television personality Jimmy Savile
travels everywhere with only one pair of underpants. (He
washes them every night, according to an interview he gave
in 2000.) I do not recommend this course of action, in line
with my overall policy of not recommending that people
model their lives on Jimmy Savile's. But you can't fault the
man for not travelling light.

I thought of Jimmy Savile's underpants (much as I try not
to) when I came across onebag.com, an extraordinary website
written by a marketing executive, Doug Dyment, whose
urbane and friendly tone belies the steely single-mindedness
of his ambition, which is never to travel anywhere with more
than a single carry-on bag, and to persuade anybody who'll
listen to do the same. Dyment's approach is intensely practical
but, taken along with other sites and books on the topic, you
can begin to perceive the outlines of a Zen-like philosophy
of travel, according to which lightweight physical baggage is
not just a metaphor for, but a cause of, a calm and happy
mind.

Dyment quotes Frank Lloyd Wright: 'To know what to
leave out and what to put in; just where and just how, ah,
that is to have been educated in the knowledge of simplicity.'
The most useful part of his site is the 'just how' – specifically,
an idiosyncratic technique called 'bundle wrapping', which
involves wrapping your clothes around each other to eliminate
air pockets, prevent creasing, and fit far more into a small
space. You'll need to consult his diagrams to try it for yourself
and, if travelling with a companion, you'll also need to learn

to withstand withering looks as you unpeel your shirts from your jeans. But it works. 'People overpack because of timidity and fear of the unknown, both largely results of inexperience,' argues Dyment, who also provides numerous tips for reducing the number of items carried, including doing laundry en route, complete with retractable washing line.

Draconian restrictions on cabin baggage in our acutely security-conscious era – no liquids except in tiny quantities a small transparent bag, etcetera – do not make any of this easier, though perhaps they do at least encourage the kind of minimalism of which OneBag approves. And anyone travelling by air still has to contend with the fact that your bag will be accepted as small enough to take on board, or rejected as too large, depending entirely on which side of the bed your check-in agent got up. But since a light and well-packed bag engenders a calm mind, you won't get angry. You'll good-temperedly hand over your bag to be stowed in the hold. And when the airline ends up routing it to Bratislava by mistake, you'll merely reflect that the ultimate way to travel light, after all, is to travel with no bags whatsoever. You can always just wash the underpants you're wearing. Jimmy Savile does.

EARPLUG-WEARERS OF THE WORLD, UNITE

An uncharitable observer might argue that I'm obsessed with noise. I've spent countless hours searching for the perfect earplug. I've bought, then returned, several pairs of expensive noise-cancelling headphones. Sometimes, to stifle keyboard-hammering colleagues in offices, I've listened through headphones to recordings of white noise. I covet a noise-masking machine called the Marpac SoundScreen 980A, and once considered buying a pair of 'noise-cancelling earmuffs' designed for use on construction sites, an environment in which I spend approximately none of my time. I own a CD called *Relaxing Sounds of Nature*, which has helped combat the Enraging Sounds of Neighbours. In my defence, I like quoting Schopenhauer, from his essay *On Noise*: 'There are people [who] are not sensitive to noise; but they are just the very people who are not sensitive to argument, or thought, or poetry, or art . . . The reason of it is that the tissue of their brains is of a very rough and coarse quality.'

I've learnt two things from all this. On the one hand, I've actually discovered the perfect earplug: it's the Howard Leight Max, an orange foam number that I buy in boxes of 200 pairs. (The secret, you'll be fascinated to learn, lies in the shape of the flange.) On the other, I've had to confront the paradox of the quest for silence: the more you focus on trying to achieve quiet, the more you are bothered by noise; and the quieter you succeed in making things, the more disruptive any remaining noise becomes. I fear for the wellbeing of people behind groups such as Britain's Noise Abatement Society: they must be eternally on edge.

We know that too much noise – at levels worse than anything I've had to endure – has serious psychological consequences, especially in children. At one New York school, pupils in classrooms facing an overground subway track fell a year behind pupils elsewhere in the building; similar effects have been linked to noise from Heathrow Airport in London.[110] After 1992, when Munich closed its old airport and opened a new one, academic performance rose at schools near the old site and fell near the new facility, while pupils' stress hormone levels went in the opposite direction.[111] And that's not to mention other possible effects on physical health, which may include increased risk of heart attacks.[112]

Yet not all noise, obviously, is bad: natural sounds, like waves on the shore, are almost universally experienced as restorative. And naturalness doesn't seem to be key: white noise, too steady to sound truly natural, lulls babies to sleep even when it's not masking other noises. What my earplug-hunt was about, I finally realised, wasn't the absence of all noise, or even all non-natural noise, but the absence of noise I hadn't chosen, couldn't control, and that seemed to imply the noisemaker's contempt for me. I've lived beneath two sets of noisy neighbours in my life, but one cared about the problem, while the other didn't. The difference in my irritation levels was enormous.

On one occasion, I spent several days in the pine forests of Massachusetts. On being shown to my room, I heard a constant, loud roar from outside. Briefly I feared I'd been placed next to a busy freeway, and I prepared to get angry. Then I opened the blind: it was the wind in the pines. Suddenly, it was an entirely wonderful sound.

8

FOLLOW ME

Gurus, God-men, and Other Questionable Characters

SELF-IMPROVEMENT WITH THE
CHURCH OF SCIENTOLOGY

I'd be lying if I said I entered the Scientologists' sparkling new Life Improvement Centre in London with an open mind. It's not that I have anything against people who believe humanity's troubles began when an intergalactic ruler landed on earth 75 million years ago, imprisoning dead souls in a volcano and causing woes that can only be relieved with the expensive assistance of the Church of Scientology, it's just that – well, OK, that stuff doesn't help. But I wanted to give them the benefit of the doubt.

The centre used to be a shabby shop offering free personality tests. But Scientology has revamped it, and now it's bright and welcoming, as if to forestall the accusation that they might be a secretive cult. A smiling man in a suit smiled at me and invited me to watch a video. 'Then I'll explain some more,' he smiled. Did I mention he was smiling?

Space aliens notwithstanding, New Age kookiness isn't the problem here. The more I explore self-help, the more tolerant I become of those who believe in angels and spirit guides: they're well-meaning, mostly, and if I happen not to share their metaphors for understanding life, so be it. But Scientologists claim to be scientific. (There's a clue in the name.) My brain, the video explained, is like two video-cassette recorders, recording my life. When traumatic things happen, the good VCR switches off and the bad one on. Scientology's 'auditing' process apparently detaches the memories from the distress, whereupon the traumatised person becomes 'clear'. One person in the video provides the following scientific explanation for the process: 'Woo-hoo! It really works!'

The smiling man sat me down at an 'e-meter', the famous Scientology machine consisting of a dial with two metal cans attached by wires. I would hold a can in each hand, he explained, and an electrical charge would pass through my brain. If it hit a distressing thought, the needle would move. 'Start by thinking of a time you felt stress.' I thought of my university exams, but the needle didn't move. For a while, the smiling man said nothing. Then he said, 'Think of a time you were very sad.' I thought about a break-up, concentrating hard, but there was no movement. 'Sometimes this can take a bit of time,' he said. He didn't stop smiling.

I thought I'd better double-check that the e-meter wasn't something comically obvious, like a heat sensor, so I squeezed the cans hard. The needle shot across the dial. 'There!' the man said. 'What were you thinking of? You see. It works!' 'Interesting,' I said, which wasn't a lie. Later, he tried to enrol me in some auditing courses – he didn't try a hard sell, to be fair – and before long I was back on the street.

I hadn't been enlightened. Nor had I been sucked into a terrifying cult. But if the feeling you're after is mild bewilderment, combined with the sensation that you might just have wasted a small portion of your life, I can recommend the Life Improvement Centre.

THE ANTI-SECRET

The Secret, a self-help book that is one of the most extraordinary publishing successes of the past decade, argues that there is a single, overwhelmingly powerful secret known to all the greatest humans through history. It has 'utterly transformed the lives of every person who ever knew it'. Plato possessed this mysterious knowledge, as did Leonardo da Vinci and

Shakespeare; all guarded it obsessively, lest it become more widely known. It has been passed down the generations, from Newton to Beethoven to Einstein. Now it has been passed to the author of *The Secret*, an Australian daytime TV producer named Rhonda Byrne. So, to recap: that's Plato, Leonardo, Shakespeare, Newton, Beethoven, Einstein, and Australian daytime TV producer Rhonda Byrne. Is it just me, or is one of these names not like the others?

Perhaps it is just me: *The Secret* has sold several million copies worldwide, and a movie version on DVD has sold similarly well. Oprah Winfrey has dedicated two shows to it, and *Newsweek* has dedicated a cover; it has spent many weeks as the bestselling popular-psychology book on both sides of the Atlantic, and one of the fastest-selling in any genre. The reason is obvious: laziness. *The Secret* echoes the New Age ideas promoted by numerous other authors, but in ultra-distilled form, stripped of all vestiges of common sense. Focusing intently on what you want in life isn't just helpful, it claims: it's all you need to do. Scenes in the movie show people visualising expensive new possessions (unremitting materialism is a recurring theme) and thereby literally altering reality, so that they get them. That, apparently, is the knowledge behind Shakespeare's and Einstein's success. And there was I thinking they were just clever.

I'm sick of all this, and so I humbly present the Anti-Secret, based on hidden knowledge from, well, published scientific studies, actually:

1. Think negatively

The psychologist Julie Norem argues in her book *The Positive Power of Negative Thinking* that being a natural pessimist is perfectly compatible with living a happy life. Positive thinkers strain to convince themselves things will go well. 'Defensive pessimists' map out worst-case scenarios and thus eliminate anxiety as a barrier to action.[113]

2. Limit your choices

Too much choice makes us miserable; believing you can do anything induces paralysis. The psychologist Dan Gilbert points to research in which students were shown a selection of photographic prints and allowed to choose one to keep. Those who were told their decision was final ended up liking their print more than those who were told they'd be able to change their minds later.[114]

3. Forget the cars, new homes, and jewellery

Our circumstances affect us far less than we imagine. Paraplegics and lottery winners, a year after becoming paraplegic or winning the lottery, report broadly similar happiness levels to those they felt prior to their life-changing experience.[115] About 50 per cent of your happiness is due to genetics, says Sonja Lyubomirsky at the University of California; 40 per cent to behaviour and ways of thinking that you can influence. Circumstances account for 10 per cent.[116] The millions Byrne is raking in may not end up making her happy after all.

THE SHORT-TEMPERED SAGE OF HAWAII

The bestselling self-help guru Wayne Dyer lives on the Hawaiian island paradise of Maui. We know this because he mentions it on every other page of his books, frequently irrelevantly. But don't imagine that Dyer can't empathise with suffering: bad things happen on Maui, too.

Twice a week, for example, a team of gardeners tends his lawns with mowers that make 'thunderous noises'. This made him angry, he says in his book *There's a Spiritual Solution to Every Problem*, until he learned to 'send a silent blessing' when they arrive, which calms him down. When he leaves Maui on speaking tours, things get worse: in one terribly upsetting anecdote, Dyer recalls how he once couldn't get a sandwich delivered to his hotel room because room service was closed. He teetered on the brink of rage, but remembered what he'd told an audience the previous day – 'Don't put your thoughts and life energy on what you don't want' – took a deep breath and went downstairs for a sandwich instead. Who said the world is running out of heroes?

Dyer's rags-to-Maui tale began in 1976 when, as a young psychotherapist, he published *Your Erroneous Zones*, a down-to-earth work of pop psychology; when it didn't sell, he travelled the US, hassling bookshops and giving radio interviews until it became a hit. He has produced more than 30 books since, each less down-to-earth than the last, along with CDs, TV shows and decks of 'affirmation cards'. In a spirit of journalistic self-sacrifice, I've been ploughing through some of them, but having done so, I have less grasp of Dyer's message, or the reasons for his popularity, than when I started.

Dyer's recent books, such as *The Power of Intention* and *Being in Balance*, swing confusingly between borrowings from eastern spirituality, with some Christianity thrown in, and an approach reminiscent of the 'law of attraction' outlined in *The Secret*, involving 'energy fields' used to 'attract' (to quote another Dyer title) 'what you really, really, really, really want'. Never mind that the Buddhist and Taoist texts he cites argue that clinging to the idea of 'what you really want' – and believing you'd be happy if you could get it – is what causes unhappiness. Dyer hides the contradictions under a concept he calls 'plugging into the Source', a cosmic power that's a bit like God, but also like electricity, and exists to give you What You Want.

I don't mind the corny tone. And many of Dyer's subsidiary messages – such as seeking a sense of calm independent of external circumstances – are admirable. The real problem is harder to define. Somehow, Dyer is just unconvincing: his own happiness seems fragile; his written style is oddly frenetic. In the examples he uses from his own life, he's always on the verge of losing the 'peace' he celebrates. The message is not the messenger, of course. But if your philosophy of happiness can only narrowly stop you exploding when room service won't bring you a sandwich, even when you're on a lecture tour to spread that very philosophy . . . mightn't it be time for some introspection?

EMOTIONAL ACUPUNCTURE

It strikes me that a basic requirement of anything calling itself a self-help technique – as opposed to, say, a scam – is that you ought to be able to do it yourself. If you have to pay someone a large sum of money before they'll reveal their secret methods, this is called something different, such as 'being an idiot'. (Although I accept that one can take this emphasis on doing it for yourself too far. 'I went to a bookstore,' says the great deadpan comedian Steven Wright, 'and I asked the saleswoman, "Where's the self-help section?" She said if she told me it would defeat the purpose.')

That's one of the things that's so intriguing about Emotional Freedom Techniques, or EFT, a crazy-sounding system from California that's gaining ground in Britain and America: it's all there, at no cost, on the website of its founder, Gary Craig, at eftuniverse.com. Which is just as well, since it involves tapping yourself repeatedly on your face and chest while reciting slogans – thus earning it the accolade of being the only thing I've felt embarrassed to do alone in a room. 'It is an emotional version of acupuncture, except needles aren't necessary,' Craig says. 'This common-sense approach draws its power from time-honoured eastern discoveries.'

You certainly can pay money for advanced EFT, carried out by professional practitioners, if you choose, and maybe their approach is different. But the charming, uncharlatanlike thing about Craig is that he makes extraordinarily ambitious claims for his method and implies you can achieve results in minutes – and for free. It can, he says, cure phobias, ease physical pain, eliminate negative emotions, improve your ability at mathematics and transform your golf game. You don't even need to believe that it will work in order for it to do so.

Naturally, I set about testing it, tapping myself in an effort to a) stop procrastinating, b) get better at mental arithmetic, having first timed myself doing a set of basic multiplication sums, and c) eliminate a persistent pain in my right knee. ('Even though I have this pain in my knee,' Craig required me to say as I tapped my eyebrows, chin and collarbone, 'I deeply and completely accept myself.')

Which brings me to a dilemma. If I'm honest, I think EFT is probably nonsense: though it's available on the National Health Service in Britain, peer-reviewed studies have not offered convincing support. Its success probably relies on distraction, since the tapping is so complicated that it interrupts any stream of depressing thoughts. The sceptic in me is supposed to be outraged by this, and if EFT promoted itself as an alternative to conventional treatment for serious illness, I would be. But if what it's mainly doing is making people feel that they're better at golf, or happier at work, or a little less achy, well, I'm disinclined to start getting all Richard Dawkins about it.

Personally, I found myself procrastinating less, very slightly faster at maths, and exactly as pained as before in my knee. I've never played golf, but for all I know I'm brilliant at it now.

HOW TO BE LIKED

Recently, for the purposes of research, I attended a workshop that promised to teach me secret techniques to make me more likeable. I wasn't thrilled at spending the day with the kind of people who would feel the need to learn these skills. Megalomaniacs? Tragic, friendless loners? (I, of course, was there for the purpose of research, just so we're clear on that.) In fact, almost everyone seemed strikingly well-adjusted. They were entrepreneurs, and executives, and a presenter from a cable television shopping channel, who was delightful, and who at no point attempted to sell me a gold-effect necklace with a pendant in the shape of Princess Diana's head.

The self-improvement world is obsessed with the tricks of rapport – clearly, they're invaluable in sales, or dating, or politics – but they're impossible even to talk about without sounding seedy and manipulative. This doesn't seem to be a problem for a certain breed of guru: 'With rapport, the world bends to your whims!' promises Keith Livingston, one such teacher, in his promotional materials. 'Communicate on an unconscious level with everyone you meet to get what you want, when you want it!' But all that felt a long way from the seminar room in central London, where Robbie and Ed, of NLP School Europe, who teach the techniques of neurolinguistic programming, were anxious to prove you could be decent and non-overbearing – British, you might call it – and still learn the arts of human interaction. 'You cannot not communicate,' as a poster on the wall declared. And so, our personable hosts explained, you might as well learn to do it well.

We spent a lot of time 'mirroring'. The TV presenter told me about her job, and I tried to copy her movements and expressions as she spoke. The theory is that all this creates a barely conscious feeling of empathy. Mostly, it created a feeling of being ridiculous, but when I tested it later in the real world, the effect was remarkable. (Try it; it's fun.) I managed to get absurdly precise in my copying, yet no one ever noticed. Then I'd walk away, cackling quietly to myself.

A lot of getting people to like you, though, is just about being a decent and generous sort of person. Research on the phenomenon of 'trait transfer' has found that if you gossip about someone for having an affair, for example, your listeners are more likely subconsciously to think of you as untrustworthy. If you praise someone as talented and generous, those qualities attach themselves to you.[117] Deciding to do this consciously isn't intrinsically manipulative, even if being liked is your goal, and it's surely positively altruistic to behave in such a way that people enjoy, rather than hate, the experience of talking to you. The deeper problem is the state of absolute mental confusion into which I'm plunged whenever I try to hold a conversation and, at the same time, measure and modify my own contributions to it. I suspect this comes with practice. Or maybe it's just a personal failing – one more reason the world is never going to bend to my whims.

THE LUCKIEST NUMBER

If you were to take all the self-help books in existence, boil them up in a big stew, then reduce the bubbling broth to a pure, intense, concentrated Essence of Self-Help Book, the result would be Jacqueline Leo's book, *Seven: The Number for Happiness, Love, and Success*. It is *The Seven Habits of Highly Effective People* meets *The Seven Spiritual Laws of Success* meets *The Seven Principles for Making Marriage Work*, plus the insights of any other guru who has ever presented advice in a list of seven, which is a lot more than seven of them. Seven, Leo contends, governs our lives in profound ways. Our very bodies are replaced every seven years, the book notes – a claim I had dismissed as highly suspect, but the authority cited by Leo is Christina Ricci, so I suppose it must be true.

The numerological fixation with seven, of course, is largely a matter of confirmation bias. Start looking, and you'll find it everywhere: seven seas, seven days of the week, seven deadly sins, seven dwarves, Shakespeare's seven ages of man, the seven natural notes in an octave. Leo even chucks in the drink 7 Up, the movie *Seven*, and the seven members of a water polo team. While reading her book, I happened to glance at my watch, and – oh, my God, this is so spooky – there was a number seven on it, right between the six and the eight!

But I'm being unfair. Even imaginary significance exerts an influence if enough people believe it, and Leo shows that cultures and religions from Mesopotamia to Hinduism to Christianity have all found the number deeply meaningful. And she marshals a sliver of *bona fide* psychological research to bolster her case: George Miller's venerable 1956 paper 'The Magical Number Seven, Plus or Minus Two: Some Limits on Our Capacity for Processing Information'.[118] 'My problem,' Miller writes, 'is that I have been persecuted by an integer. For seven years this number has followed me around, has intruded in my most private data, and has assaulted me from the pages of our most public journals.' One of his conclusions is that seven – or rather seven-ish, as his title suggests – is so ubiquitous in life because it represents the largest number of items, such as numbers or words, that the average person can retain in short-term memory. Seven does, in a sense, structure the way we encounter the world. Leo calls it 'a natural brain filter', something particularly crucial in an era of information onslaught. Her various lists of seven – ways to live simply, ways to eat healthily, and so on, which are full of good ideas – could just as easily be nine or fifteen items long, but then you wouldn't remember them.

As self-help prescriptions go, using seven to govern your life seems comically arbitrary. But arbitrary rules, providing they're recognised for what they are, can be some of the best. You don't need a supernatural reason for adopting a personal rule to contact seven of your friends each week, or tick seven items off your to-do list each day. If the rule gives rise to action, that's enough. No mystery required.

Still – seven colours in the rainbow, seven bones in the neck of a giraffe, and, Leo informs us, Nicolas Cage gets a new tattoo every seven years . . . You can't help but wonder. I mean, what are the chances?

HOW TO BE A GENUINE FAKE

The wild-eyed Armenian-born mystic George Ivanovich Gurdjieff, who died in 1949, was once described by *Time* magazine as 'a remarkable blend of P.T. Barnum, Rasputin, Freud, Groucho Marx and everybody's grandfather', which is one of those phrases that means less the more you ponder it. It tells us – what? That he was part showman, part amoral charlatan, part deeply insightful student of psychology and part joker, and that he probably had some facial hair (which he did: a splendid handlebar moustache). But perhaps *Time*'s lack of precision was appropriate. The natural urge, confronted with those deemed to be spiritual gurus, is to categorise. Was

Gurdjieff a sincere and earnest teacher – like, say, the Buddhist writer Thich Nhat Hanh, to pick an uncontroversial example – or a fraudster and cult leader? Yet, like many of the mystical types inhabiting the borderlands between self-help and spirituality, Gurdjieff presents a challenge. Was he the real thing, or a fake? It's not just that the question is hard to answer. It's that when you really look closely at the man behind the moustache, it starts to seem like the wrong question.

Gurdjieff's essential message was that humanity is asleep, and he seems to have meant it almost literally: that most of life, whether we're talking warfare or grocery shopping, is undertaken so automatically that we might as well be – indeed, might actually be – in an unconscious trance. 'A modern man lives in sleep, in sleep he is born, and in sleep he dies,' Gurdjieff said, and his mission was to wake people up, frequently by shouting at them ('Do you want to die like dogs?'). According to legend, his follower and chief biographer P.D. Ouspensky only really grasped the guru's point when he saw a truckload of artificial limbs being supplied, in advance of hostilities, to troops in the First World War. Something clicked in his mind: here was a society so robotic that, instead of halting the slide to war, it was calmly provisioning itself for war's destruction. The Gurdjieff technique known as 'the stop exercise' aimed at inducing a similar click. When he shouted 'Stop!', followers were to freeze and examine their mental, emotional and physical states, and ask themselves if, up until that moment, they'd been acting on autopilot, sleepwalking through the day.

This is a good point, and it remains a good point even when you learn of the troubling cult of personality that grew around Gurdjieff, the celebrity acolytes he bewitched, and his reputation for sleeping with female followers. It's not just that he was a flawed man preaching a good message. Rather, it was that the question posed by his every action and pronouncement – is this man real, or a fake? – was exactly what made him valuable, whether he knew it or not. For if the suggestion being made is that daily life is indeed somehow dreamlike (not just Gurdjieff's claim, but the claim of all gurus preaching the possibility of 'enlightenment' or 'awakening'), then focusing on the question of what's 'real' or 'fake' is the whole point. This isn't to excuse cynical fraud. But if a spiritual showman like Gurdjieff, by the very act of walking the tightrope between the two, prompts you to ask questions where previously you made assumptions, his job is done. He has shouted 'Stop!', and you've stopped.

'My own feeling has always been that in order to be a real person you must know how to be a genuine fake,' wrote the 1960s counterculture philosopher Alan Watts, who enjoyed referring to himself as a 'put-on', and probably wouldn't have minded accusations of charlatanry. He meant that it was vital to become aware that so much of life was a charade – a web of shared assumptions, of conventions most people performed robotically – precisely in order to enjoy playing the charade, and thus to really live. For Watts, a mystic like Gurdjieff, those questionable shared assumptions included selfhood itself: we're all part of a cosmic whole, he insisted, and our belief in our own separate selves is part of the charade. All that mattered was not to forget that it was a performance. 'I am unashamedly in "showbiz",' he observed of his life spent writing and speaking on spiritual themes. So was Gurdjieff. 'But' – Watts's crucial coda – 'so is everyone.'

SYSTEMS FOR SUCCESS

'Can there really be a system for success?' asks the insurance salesman turned positive-thinking guru W. Clement Stone

in his 1960s classic, *The Success System That Never Fails*.
(Perspicacious readers may infer his answer to the question
from the book's title.) Stone belongs to a bygone era: a pencil-
moustached, bow-tied bundle of energy, he made employees
of his insurance firm chant 'I feel ter-r-rific!' each morning,
yet spent vast chunks of his fortune propping up the career
of America's least smiley president, Richard Nixon. But one
thing that hasn't changed since those days is self-help's obsession
with systems. Want to make big money telling people how
to change their lives? You've got to have a system.

Anyone can dispense advice. To present your advice as a
system, as almost every pop-psychology star from Deepak
Chopra to Stephen Covey does, is to make grander claims:
that it's a comprehensive solution, and that if you master its
details – which are unique to the system, of course – success
is guaranteed. Good advice is usually simple and timeworn; a
lucrative system should be complex and purportedly new. It's
a question of branding: relatively few people will pay much
money, for example, to be told that gratitude makes you happier,
though that's a potentially transformative insight. Concoct a
Gratitude System™ full of intricate routines and jargon, by
contrast, and they'll not only pay for it: they'll spend more
money, later, for your Gratitude System Thankfulness
Workbook, even though it's just a cheap notepad with a fancy
cover.

The whispered promise of such systems is that they'll render
self-improvement automatic, bridging the excruciating gap
between knowing how to change and actually changing. Here,
at last, is the sequence of strategies that will let you lose weight
without self-discipline, or the time-management method that
will spare you from confronting the fact that you're simply
overcommitted. But the awkward truth is that it's almost never
the details that matter. When diets work, they may well do

so largely because limiting your calorie intake works, not because lemon juice, or cabbage soup, or a specific carbs-to-protein ratio is the previously undiscovered secret to health.

It's not just self-help. For decades, psychotherapists have argued the merits of their different schools (Freudian, Jungian, cognitive, and so on), while cynics have doubted the efficacy of therapy altogether. Then, in 2001, a study led by the psychologist Bruce Wampold shocked everyone. Therapy was definitely effective, he found – often much more than drugs – but the kind of therapy was almost irrelevant: specific techniques accounted for less than 1 per cent of variance in improvement rates among patients. What mattered wasn't their particular system, but whether they were competent and trusted by clients.[119]

As for Clement Stone, he surely didn't make millions because of a Success System That Never Fails, but because he was relentless, lucky and stubbornly determined to get rich: he tried many things, over and over, and some worked. After all, if success could be reduced to an infallible step-by-step system, couldn't Nixon have employed it, too?

9

ROADS LESS TRAVELLED

Some Unlikely Paths to Happiness

THE BENEFITS OF MEDIOCRITY

Let me be frank – what I'm about to say here is probably going to be pretty mediocre. In case your response is 'So what's new?', I ought to explain: this time, I'm doing it deliberately. Partly, this may just be a petty rebellion against popular psychology's impossible perfectionism. But there was another, more immediate cause – a news story in the London *Evening Standard* about a team of management consultants forcing civil servants to stick black tape on their desks, marking out precisely where their computers, staplers, pens and packed lunches should go. Now, I'm as much of a fan of tidiness as the next person, but that pushed me over the edge and into the arms of imperfectionism, and the joys of doing things badly.

'I dare you to try to be "average",' the cognitive therapist David Burns writes in his bestseller *Feeling Good*. 'Does the prospect seem blah and boring? Very well – I dare you to try it for just one day . . . I predict two things will happen. First, you won't be particularly successful at being 'average'. Second, in spite of this, you will receive substantial satisfaction from what you do. More than usual.' His point being that perfectionism isn't just a rather stressful way of being brilliant – the kind of trait you might secretly be proud of – but that in the end it's a path to achieving less, as well as not enjoying the experience. 'Try for 80%, 60% or 40%. Then see how much you enjoy the activity, and how productive you are.'

You could extract a similar message from *A Perfect Mess: The Hidden Benefits of Disorder*, an almost indecently fascinating book by Eric Abrahamson and David Freedman. The costs of trying to maintain a highly ordered system often outweigh the benefits, they say. A messy desk, like Einstein's, can be 'a highly effective prioritising and accessing system', since it will develop an emergent structure modelled on how your specific mind works, not some externally imposed schema. And did you know there's at least one firm that makes money out of adding background noise to mobile-phone conversations, because perfect silence fazes people? Turning to imperfect housekeeping, the authors make much of the discovery of penicillin (the ultimate, unanswerable argument against doing the dishes). And they offer the following tip: 'Making a bed when you get up in the morning is like tying a shoe after you've taken it off' – a statement that gets more philosophically profound, and more existentially troubling, the longer you reflect upon it.

There are signs that all this may be catching on, for example in websites championing 'imperfect parenting', and in the work of the US design guru Dan Ho, whose book *Rescue from Domestic Perfection* rails against obsessive attempts to impose perfect order, and the underlying psychological tendencies they expose.

At this point, normally, I'd expend much effort trying to think of a funny ending, or a stylish summation of the foregoing paragraphs, but you know what? Screw it.

WHAT IF THERE ACTUALLY ISN'T A PROBLEM?

In 2010, the American Psychiatric Association released the provisional results of its long-term effort to update the *Diagnostic and Statistical Manual*, the thousand-page tome that classifies every mental disorder in existence, and thus effectively dictates what counts as a disorder and what doesn't.[120] It's been a decade of bitter, shrink-on-shrink infighting. For example, how much sex is 'excessive', indicating addiction? Are we talking Warren Beatty levels, or just enough to make APA members jealous? Is shopaholism really a sickness? And so on.

We're inclined to think of illnesses as objective: either you have one or you don't. But the DSM shows how subjective things are. Under the new proposals, Asperger's syndrome would simply vanish, its symptoms reclassified as a form of autism, just because a committee of psychiatrists decreed it. Until 1973, homosexuality was defined as a disorder. Today, critics fear that moody teenagers (in other words, teenagers) may find themselves classified as suffering 'temper dysregulation'. All of which underlines a point with implications far beyond psychiatry: we spend our days trying to fix problems – at work, in our personal lives, in politics – but rarely stop to consider how something gets defined as a problem in the first place.

Curiously, the canniest insight into this may have come from Bert Lance, once a senior adviser to Jimmy Carter. Lance is an unlikely source of spiritual wisdom – he was forced to resign amid allegations of corruption, though he was later acquitted – yet it was he who brought to prominence, in 1977, a then-obscure Southern proverb: 'If it ain't broke, don't fix it.' 'That's the trouble with government,' Lance told a magazine interviewer. 'Fixing things that aren't broken, and not fixing things that are broken.'

It's not only government. This is also the unspoken assumption of self-help culture, of every company that ever called in the consultants to help it find a new direction, and of countless other projects for change: that something needs fixing, and that we know what that something is. A book or workshop on becoming more assertive (or productive, or richer) may offer good or bad advice on fixing that problem – but don't expect it to challenge your belief that you've got a problem, or that it's the one you think it is. And 'fixing', in reality, may not just be futile; it may make things worse. As the anthropologist Gregory Bateson pointed out, picking one aspect of a complex system and relentlessly trying to improve it can lead to disaster if you ignore all the other interconnected elements. Why assume, say, that your company should make ever greater profits? We don't assume a vitamin-deficient person should eat ever more fruit; after a point, other problems will arise as a by-product of trying to maximise just one element.

There's a risk of glibness here, especially when it comes to people in serious psychological distress: they really do have a problem – the distress itself – and telling them they don't is both heartless and pointless. But that doesn't mean the problem is what they imagine it to be. 'We are surrounded by therapies and diets and self-improvement programs, all of which promise to fix us,' notes the psychotherapist and Zen teacher Barry Magid in *Ending the Pursuit of Happiness*. 'What we don't realise is the way all of them tacitly reinforce our assumption that we are broken and need fixing. What if . . . we really deeply challenged that assumption once and for all?' Perhaps the problem, sometimes, is the notion that there's a problem.

STOP LOOKING WHERE YOU'RE GOING

My favourite anecdote about the novelist Anthony Trollope – no less noteworthy, I like to think, for also being my only anecdote about Anthony Trollope – concerns his writing habits. Each morning, before leaving for his job at the post office, he wrote for three hours. ('Three hours a day,' he reckoned, 'will produce as much as a man ought to write.') So far, so disciplined. But here's the kicker: if he finished a novel midway through a three-hour period, he just started writing the next one. Say what you like about his writing, but he wasn't one for mooning around the house, complaining of creative exhaustion. 'My novels, whether good or bad, have been as good as I could make them,' he reflected. 'Had I taken three months of idleness between each, they would have been no better.'

It's easy to see this as indicative of workaholism, or of a dull, unimaginative, grinder's attitude; critics have certainly disdained Trollope for producing too many words and not enough art. But there's something useful to be learned here, too – not from Trollope's relentlessness, but from his focus on process rather than outcome. His goal, it appears (though of course we can only guess), wasn't 'finish great book', or even 'get paid'. It was 'put in three hours'. Exactly what did or didn't result from all those three-hour chunks, he seems to have recognised, was beyond his control and not worth worrying about.

Admittedly, there's something about this that rankles. Working on an assembly line is boring, and the post-industrial era promises an escape from such soul-crushing routinisation. Why, then, would anyone voluntarily turn creative work into an assembly line, which is effectively what Trollope was doing? Besides, paying no attention to outcomes runs counter to much prevailing wisdom: companies encourage employees to set goals; business gurus preach 'outcome-oriented thinking'; the self-help luminary Stephen Covey urges us to 'begin with the end in mind'. Every book on living the life of your dreams requires that you visualise your desired end point in detail, then work towards it.

And yet, as the sports psychologist John Eliot points out in his book *Overachievement*, 'nothing discourages the concentration necessary to perform well . . . more than worrying about the outcome'. The marathon runner who's reached a state of 'flow' isn't visualising the finish line, but looking through a narrower lens, focusing on one stride, then another, then another. This isn't merely a matter of breaking a big project into chunks, which is an adjustment of scale; rather, it's a total shift in perspective. The young Jerry Seinfeld's scriptwriting technique involved marking an X on a calendar for every day he sat and typed. His goal was nothing more than an unbroken chain of Xs. If he'd aimed instead to write brilliant jokes, he'd have been distracted and intimidated.

But to see this as a mere productivity trick is to miss Eliot's point. We can't control outcomes in any sphere of life. All you can do – and therefore the only responsibility you have – is to put in the time and effort: into relationships, parenting, finding happiness, whatever. The actual result, in a profound sense, is none of your business. Take this one step further, and it becomes positively meditative: a matter, in the words of the Vietnamese Buddhist monk Thich Nhat Hanh, of 'doing the dishes just to do the dishes', not to achieve clean dishes. Which is an outlook on life in general that's worth considering, even if you own a dishwasher.

TO BE, OR NOT TO BE?

Halfway through the 1960s, the author David Bourland published an essay proposing a radical overhaul of English based on eliminating all forms of the verb 'to be'.[121] In a world where we all spoke E-Prime, as Bourland called this new language, you couldn't say 'Sandra Bullock's latest film is shockingly mediocre'; you'd have to say it 'seems mediocre to me'. Shakespeare productions would need retooling ('To live or not to live, I ask this question'), as would the Bible ('The Lord functions as my shepherd'). The world, in short, would feel very different – though in E-Prime you couldn't actually say it 'was' very different. Unsurprisingly, it proved even less popular than Esperanto, and in fairness Bourland never meant it as a serious replacement for English. But his eccentric vision deserves celebrating. Because in theory at least, E-Prime aimed at nothing less than using language to make our insane lives a little more sane.

Bourland studied under Alfred Korzybski, a Polish aristocrat and émigré who founded the philosophy of General Semantics, made famous by his slogan, 'The map is not the territory.' To think about and function in the world, Korzybski said, we rely on systems of abstract concepts, most obviously language. But those concepts don't reflect the world in a straightforward way; instead, they contain hidden traps that distort reality, causing confusion and angst. And the verb 'to be', he argued, contains the most traps of all.

Take the phrase, 'My brother is lazy'. It seems clear, but Korzybski and Bourland would say it deceives: it implies certainty and objectivity, when in reality it expresses an opinion. Even, 'The sky is blue' papers over the details: I really mean, 'The sky appears blue to me'. 'Our judgments can only be probabilistic,' said Allen Walker Read, a Korzybski follower, in a paper entitled 'Language Revisions by the Deletion of Absolutisms'. 'Therefore we would do well to avoid finalistic, absolutistic terms. Can we ever find "perfection" or "certainty" or "truth"? No! Then let us stop using such words in our formulations.' E-Prime provided an easy way to do this: simply stop using 'to be'.

All this might seem maniacally pointless pedantry. But as cognitive therapists note, thoughts trigger emotions, and 'finalistic, absolutistic' thoughts trigger stressful emotions. 'I am a failure' feels permanent, all-encompassing, hopeless. Restating it in E-Prime – 'I feel like a failure', or 'I have failed at this task' – makes it limited, temporary, addressable.

'I have found repeatedly,' wrote the novelist Robert Anton Wilson, an E-Prime advocate, 'that when baffled by a problem in science, in philosophy, or in daily life, I gain immediate insight by writing down what I know about the enigma in strict E-Prime.' Political debates might benefit, too, since E-Prime renders unyielding dogmatism – 'All immigrants are scroungers!', 'Taxation is theft!', etcetera – essentially impossible. As George Santayana put it, 'The little word "is" has its tragedies.'

E-Prime never really caught on; General Semantics fell out of fashion. (It can't have helped that Korzybski's fans included that high-priest of nonsense, L. Ron Hubbard.) Even so, trying to express one's thoughts without using 'to be' can have a curiously salutary, bracing effect. In the preceding paragraphs, with the obvious exception of the quoted examples, I have attempted to do this.

EXTREME MODERATION

Moderation doesn't sell self-help books. There's a reason why Anthony Robbins, the grinning guru famous for 'inspiring' people to walk barefoot over hot coals, called his bestseller *Awaken the Giant Within*, not *Awaken the Somewhat Taller Person Within*. Robbins advocates taking 'massive action' to make 'sweeping changes', just like he did when – can you guess? – he hit rock bottom and decided to turn his life around. 'I decided to change virtually every aspect of my life,' he writes. 'I would never again settle for less than I could be.' (Motivational speakers always have a personal back story like this, in which they hit rock bottom, then decide to change their lives by immediately becoming motivational speakers, which is, when you think about it, a bit weird.)

If there's one thing I've learnt from my journey through self-help, it's that extremism like this doesn't work. Deciding to go from couch-potato to running five miles every morning, from disorganised to blisteringly efficient, from gloomy by nature to ultra-optimistic . . . all this makes failure nearly inevitable. Then, a dispiriting spiral kicks in, where you give up, go for broke again, give up even more completely, and so on. Still, it's worth asking why this disastrous approach always seems so enticing. The clichéd answer is that these days everyone's looking for a quick fix. But most people who resolve to make some change in their lives aren't feeling lazy: on the contrary, they're feeling idealistic and energetic, however fleetingly. That's a noble feeling, not a shameful one, and it would be nice to think there was a way of harnessing it in a way that wasn't doomed to fail.

Ladies and gentlemen, I give you 'extreme moderation'. Partly, this is just an excuse to highlight the endlessly fascinating website everydaysystems.com, whose proprietor, Reinhard Engels, coined the phrase. (He's best known for inventing a crazy but effective home-fitness tool called Shovelglove, consisting of a sledgehammer with an old sweater wrapped around it.) Extremist approaches to life, Engels notes, have the virtue of clarity. If you have a drink problem, and decide never to touch another drop, your personal rule is unambiguous: there isn't a slippery slope. 'You can cross this line, if you decide,' he writes, 'but you can't do it by accident or by imperceptible degree.'

Usually, though, extremism demands too much of us: we want to cut back on drinking and still savour good beer, or go running more often without threatening our cherished weekend mornings in bed. 'The most powerful extremist technique is drawing hard, clear lines and exploding when those lines come anywhere close to being crossed,' Engels

notes. 'Moderates should be the same way – except we draw
those lines in different places.' Choose a moderate goal, then
stick to it with an extremist's zeal. Set an upper limit of x
drinks per night; cut out sugary foods three days a week; run
one mile twice weekly. You won't transform your life in seven
days, but you won't do that by reading books called *Transform
Your Life in Seven Days*, either. And at least with extreme
moderation you might make things a bit better, not worse.

GIVING UP NEVER FELT SO GOOD

Among the preposterous ideas drummed into us as children
is the notion that it's inherently good to finish what you start.
The most common manifestation of this is the 'starving children
in Africa' argument for clearing your plate – a line of reasoning
so absurd that you wonder whether being three years old was
really a good enough excuse for not getting wise to it. Next
time you hear a politician say of some disastrous venture that
it's 'important to see the job through', it's worth reflecting: is
this person just locked in some childhood psychodrama,
endlessly playing out a moment when they were rewarded
with a lollipop for finishing their food?

Several productivity experts say they've hit on a better
approach, borrowed from wartime medicine. 'Triage', in its
original form, was the battlefield surgeon's practice of quickly
dividing the wounded into three groups: the ones who'd die
even if they got medical attention, the ones who'd survive
even if they didn't get any, and the ones for whom medical
attention would make the difference between life and death.
With limited resources, it makes sense to focus on the third
group. And, if you'll pardon the tasteless transition from the
horrors of war to the 'horrors' of modern living, it sometimes

pays to approach your day-to-day existence in a broadly similar spirit. For example:

1. Email

A brutal but liberating quick fix: assume that any emails older than three weeks are 'dead' or non-essential, and scoop them into a separate folder. Now forget about them. For ever. (If the senders needed a response, they'll let you know. But they've probably forgotten, or found another solution to their problem.)

2. Half-read books

If you've neglected a book for more than two weeks, and it's on your bedside table only out of guilt, shelve it, or give it away, for example using the website bookcrossing.com.

3. Personal projects, hobbies, etcetera

The most insidious kind of to-do list clutter are the things you started only because you wanted to, not because you had to – except that now you don't want to do them any more. Junk them. 'Practising triage is extremely challenging because it requires saying "no" again and again to what you may feel are good causes,' writes the blogger Steve Pavlina, at stevepavlina.com. 'It's the time management equivalent of saying "no" to wounded people calling for help.'

4. Friends

Another piece of advice from Pavlina: if there are people you need to summon up the effort to contact every few months – if it's become a mutual chore to continue the framework of a friendship, without any substance – try stopping.

We feel bad about abandoning things – it's our childhood training – and, like children, seem to feel we need permission to do so. Therefore, as someone you have no overwhelming reason to trust or obey, I'd like to say: you have my permission. Also, I spoke to the Dalai Lama, and he said it was OK, too.

BLISSFUL IGNORANCE

When business gurus want to illustrate the dangers of unimaginative, head-in-the-sand thinking, they'll frequently quote one of History's Most Ridiculously Inaccurate Predictions. Did you know that the chairman of IBM once claimed there'd be a world market for 'maybe five computers'? Or that an internal memo at the telegraph company Western Union concluded that 'this "telephone" has too many shortcomings to be seriously considered as a means of communication'? (See also Bill Gates – '640 kilobytes ought to be enough for anybody' – and Harry Warner, of Warner Bros:'Who the hell wants to hear actors talk?') Ironically, these quotes are themselves ridiculously inaccurate: all are apocryphal, or ripped out of context. But one shouldn't complain. Dodgy anecdotes are to motivational literature as facts are to science, and in this case the point being made is a good one: in business as in life, calcified ideas about the right way to do things can be a serious obstacle to doing them well.

This has a fascinating implication: if knowledge – about the 'right way' to proceed – can be a bad thing, might it make sense to think of ignorance as a precious resource, worth stewarding? 'Unlike knowledge, which is infinitely reusable, ignorance is a one-shot deal: once it has been replaced by knowledge, it can be hard to get back,' the scholar David Gray writes in a *Harvard Business Review* article entitled 'Wanted: Chief Ignorance Officer'. 'And after it's gone, we are more apt to follow well-worn paths to find answers . . . Solved problems tend to stay solved – sometimes disastrously so.' Might imagination and a certain kind of ignorance in fact be one and the same thing? Spend time around children, more than one writer on creativity advises: kids don't yet know what's been officially deemed impossible, which puts them at an advantage. Or as Picasso put it, using slightly Cubist grammar, 'All children are artists. The problem is how to remain an artist once he grows up.'

This may be one reason why the idea of 'feedback', beloved by so many managers, so rarely works. The management scholar Charles Jacobs, in *Management Rewired*, cites studies showing that when employees get positive feedback, it usually leads to no improvement, while negative feedback makes things worse. In both cases, the focus is entirely on the past. Even in the best-case scenario, good ideas for future improvement will end up being defined in the conceptual framework of what's gone before.

If this sounds like a brainless championing of stupidity, consider it mathematically: compared with the universe of your ignorance, the terrain of your knowledge is maybe the size of Liechtenstein. And what's the probability that most of the good stuff lies within Liechtenstein's borders? It's in the shadowy world of the unknown unknowns (thank you, Donald Rumsfeld, for your single positive contribution to humanity) that the biggest dangers lie, but also the biggest opportunities. 'Most of us will cheerfully acknowledge our ignorance about plenty of things,' Gray writes. 'But few of us would dare cultivate a healthy ignorance . . . within our own fields of endeavour.'

Perhaps we should. Or perhaps I just don't know what I'm talking about. In which case, I suppose, what I've got to say may be particularly valuable.

WHEN BAD THINGS STOP

We can all agree, presumably, that learning to appreciate life's smaller pleasures – a sunset, a cup of coffee, the sight of a newborn lamb as it drinks a cup of coffee at sunset – is a highly beneficial thing. And yet there's something uniquely aggravating about being instructed, whether by books or well-meaning friends, to savour such moments. 'Run barefoot through grass!', 'Smell the morning air!', 'Relish a piece of chocolate!', we're urged. All admirable, but perhaps the problem is that we must discover our own pleasures for ourselves. Perhaps it's that the advice so often sounds smug. Or perhaps it's just that running barefoot through the park near my house would be a really, really bad idea, unless you're up for savouring the feeling of broken glass, and much worse, against the soles of your feet.

So it's always refreshing to return to the work of the Canadian author Neil Pasricha, proprietor of the blog 1000awesomethings.com. A fair number of Pasricha's reflections on everyday sources of happiness, it's true, are of the sunsets-and-lambs variety. But he also has a deep affinity for another category of pleasures, usually neglected by purveyors of pop psychology, which fall under the heading of 'relief': the joyous moment an unpleasant experience stops, or when things don't turn out half as badly as you were expecting.

Who'd dissent, for example, from Pasricha's observation that there's a weirdly disproportionate enjoyment, when hauling luggage or shopping, in 'picking up something that turns out to be a lot lighter than you expected'? Or 'dropping your cellphone on the sidewalk and then realising it's totally fine'? Or arriving late for a rendezvous, sweaty and exhausted, only to find the other person's even later? When, against all expectations, the queue you're in moves faster than the others? Or, I would add – a slightly different variety of relief – when at last you get to finish some arduous chore, or an exasperating houseguest finally leaves?

Clearly, enjoying the feelings of relief isn't a brilliant strategy for long-term fulfilment: if you're in a terrible job, or terrible relationship, it's no real justification to say it's worth it because it's nice to leave the office each day, or lovely when your partner's not around. 'Expect the worst and you'll never be disappointed' is a dispiriting way to live. On a smaller scale, though, it can be a real source of joy, and a pleasingly democratic one: we might not all have the capacity to stop, in the midst of a hellish day, to watch a sunset, but even the gloomiest among us can savour the times our gloomiest expectations are confounded, or our least favourite activities end. Indeed, isn't this one area where being downbeat is actually an advantage? If you're such a cheery optimist that you're happy whatever happens, you'll never know the thrill of having things turn out less terribly than expected.

Not long ago, the blogger Gretchen Rubin noted (at happiness-project.com) that she'd been cheered, one morning, by hearing bagpipes outside her window. At first, I was awed: I couldn't imagine being so good at appreciating the world that I'd appreciate even bagpipes. But then I realised that I, too, am grateful for bagpipe-playing buskers, albeit for different reasons. Because without them, I'd never experience that moment – exquisite, cherishable, infinitely tranquil – when they stop.

EMBRACE IMPERFECTION

The Roman emperor Marcus Aurelius, when not waging war against the Parthians, had a fondness for crusty bread – the kind we might call 'artisanal', though back then he probably just called it bread. 'When bread is baked,' he observes in *The Meditations*, 'some parts are split at the surface, and these . . . have a certain fashion contrary to the purpose of the baker's art, are beautiful . . . and in a peculiar way excite a desire for eating.' It's precisely the irregularities that stimulate the appetite. Similarly, he adds, figs 'gape open' deliciously when almost overripe. Clearly, had he been born two millennia later, Marcus could have operated a chain of criminally overpriced north London delicatessens selling peasant-style cheeses, olives and chutneys. What a missed opportunity. What a waste of talent.

We live now, of course, in an era obsessed with the artisanal and rustic. 'Everything the old gentry tried to make smooth, we in today's educated gentry try to make rough,' the columnist David Brooks notes in his well-observed book *Bobos in Paradise*. 'They covered ceiling beams. We expose them. They buried bulky stone chimneys in plaster . . . [We] admire massive rocky hearths.' Smoothness is out; roughness is in.

There's much about this that's preposterous – it leads rich people to spend vast sums on stuff that looks cheap, while being vaguely insulting towards actual peasants – but it has a kernel of something worthwhile, crystallised in a Japanese term that increasingly crops up in Anglophone discussions on everything from art to self-help: *wabi-sabi*. Defining this precisely is beyond me but, broadly, it's the aesthetic that finds beauty in imperfection and transience: in buildings beaten by wind and rain; in rough-hewn objects that hint at their inevitable decay; in the asymmetrical, chipped, off-kilter pottery used in the Japanese tea ceremony.

'It is a beauty of things imperfect, impermanent, and incomplete,' writes Leonard Koren, in *Wabi-Sabi for Artists, Designers, Poets & Philosophers*. 'It is a beauty of things modest and humble.' His near-namesake, Leonard Cohen, gets closer to the heart of things: 'Forget your perfect offering/There's a crack in everything/That's how the light gets in.' This isn't merely 'accepting' imperfection, as countless lifestyle gurus would have us do. Instead, the imperfection is the point.

Sceptics needn't think of this as some wishy-washy spiritual insight. Absolute flawlessness, it's long been observed, is disturbing. It offers no point of connection, and may help explain the 'uncanny valley' effect, where almost-lifelike robots trigger revulsion in humans. 'Nothing is ever perfect; even when it appears so, we are subconsciously looking for the flaw,' observes the marketing researcher Martin Lindstrom, writing in *Fast Company*. Likewise, symmetry and perfect ratios seem to be crucial for facial attractiveness – yet, at the extremes, such findings start to diverge from our real experience of beauty: one study last year concluded that Shania Twain had the perfect face, according to strict measures of symmetry, with Angelina Jolie trailing behind.[122]

Even imperfection can be pursued perfectionistically, to be sure: there's nothing remotely *wabi-sabi* about spending thousands on a slate countertop that's irregular in exactly the right way. If you really found beauty in flawedness, perhaps you'd hang on to the Formica one.

FURTHER ADVENTURES IN POPULAR PSYCHOLOGY

Additional Reading and Resources

Some of the web addresses included here are long. To avoid manually typing them into your browser, visit oliverburkeman.com/helplinks.htm, where they are listed as clickable links.

1

CHANGE EVERYTHING, RIGHT NOW!: A SHORT TOUR OF SELF-HELP'S BIGGEST CLICHÉS

On **the perils of perfectionism**, Anne Lamott's book *Bird by Bird: Some Instructions on Writing and Life* (Anchor) is well worth reading, whether or not you're interested in writing; if you *are* interested in writing, take special note of her chapter entitled 'Shitty First Drafts'. Lamott's witty yet forgiving outlook – inflected with religion, but not in a way that need distress unreligious readers – is an excellent antidote to self-help's strenuous preoccupation with total change. A half-hour video interview with her is available online at bigthink.com/ideas/19807.

Cal Newport's original blog post on the problems with **finding your passion** is at calnewport.com/blog/2009/ 11/24, and it's the kind of topic that crops up frequently on his blog Study Hacks (calnewport.com/blog) and in his book *How to Be a High School Superstar* (Broadway) – both of which, despite their titles, contain plenty of content relevant to non-students. For a well-reasoned counterpoint, see Ken Robinson's *The Element: How Finding Your Passion Changes Everything* (Penguin). And for more on the notion of **leaving your comfort zone**, explore the Japanese psychotherapy of Shoma Morita at todoinstitute.org. Morita therapy, roughly speaking, is what you get when you cross Zen Buddhism with Susan Jeffers's book *Feel the Fear and Do It Anyway* (Vermilion). In a good way.

Much of the writing **against goal-setting** also comes from a Buddhist or Taoist perspective – see, for example, Alan Watts's idiosyncratic *Tao: The Watercourse Way* (Pantheon) – while Leo Babauta gives his own take at Zen Habits (zenhabits.net/no-goal), a compelling blog on minimalist, stress-free lifestyles. For a more scholarly take on the matter, see the Harvard Business School study 'Goals Gone Wild: The Systematic Side-Effects of Over-Prescribing Goal Setting', downloadable at hbswk.hbs.edu/item/6114.html.

Broader **critiques of self-help** tend to fall into the same all-or-nothing trap as self-help itself: while too many gurus claim everything is possible with positive thinking and a ten-step checklist, too many critics dismiss the entire industry. But both Steve Salerno's *Sham: How the Gurus of the Self-Help Movement Make Us Helpless* (Nicholas Brealey) and Barbara Ehrenreich's more recent *Smile or Die: How Positive Thinking Fooled America and the World* (Granta) are sharp and illuminating. The sceptical self-help blog Beyond Growth (beyondgrowth.net) comes closest to finding a fruitful middle way.

2
HOW TO BE HAPPIER: EMOTIONAL LIFE

The definitive book on **the psychology of gratitude** is *Thanks! How Practising Gratitude Can Make You Happier* (Houghton Mifflin Harcourt) by Robert Emmons, while many research papers on the topic, by Emmons, Michael McCullough and others, are downloadable in PDF format at www.psy.miami.edu/faculty/mmccullough/Gratitude_Page.htm. A thousand websites purport to explain 'how to keep a gratitude journal', but they boil down to this: list five or six things you're grateful for. In a notebook. And repeat. (They need not be major things, either, and might include the sandwich you had for lunch.) Sonja Lyubomirsky, in *The How of Happiness: A Practical Guide to Getting the Life You Want* (Sphere), makes the interesting point that, according to some research, it may be more effective to keep such a journal intermittently, rather than day after day, so that the technique itself doesn't fall victim to the 'hedonic treadmill'.

On **worry**, Edward Hallowell's book *Worry* (Ballantine) provides the best marriage of research to practical advice; it also contains a marvellous chapter on the chronic worrying of Samuel Johnson – who, despite being one of the biggest overachievers in English history, considered himself a 'castle of indolence'. What better evidence that the intensity of a worry may be an unreliable indicator that there is a serious problem?

Jamie Pennebaker offers a list of practical tips on the link between **writing and mental health** at homepage.psy.utexas. edu/homepage/faculty/pennebaker/home2000/Writingand Health.html. One intriguing elaboration of these ideas is the technique known as 'proprioceptive writing', described at pwriting.org and in the book *Writing the Mind Alive* (Ballantine), by Linda Trichter Metcalf and Simon Tobin. And on the much-debated topic of **whether having children really makes you happy**, you'll read no more absorbing journalistic treatment of the research than Jennifer Senior's *New York* magazine article 'All Joy and No Fun: Why Parents Hate Parenting', at nymag.com/news/features/67024.

How to Live on 24 Hours a Day, Arnold Bennett's funny short book on **the benefits of paying attention** – and much else besides – is available in full online at gutenberg.org/etext/2274. For more on the **psychological benefits of nature**, it's worth going back to the source, Henry

David Thoreau's highly readable *Walden* (Oxford, or many other editions). Mark Coleman's *Awake in the Wild: Mindfulness in Nature as a Path to Self-Discovery* (New World Library) puts a more explicitly Buddhist spin on similar ideas. But forget books; may I recommend going for a walk?

Loneliness and solitude – and the very significant differences between them – are explored in John Cacioppo's *Loneliness: Human Nature and the Need for Social Connection* (Norton), as well as in Anthony Storr's *Solitude* (Flamingo) and *Party of One: The Loners' Manifesto* (Avalon) by Anneli Rufus. Emily White's *Lonely: A Memoir* (HarperCollins) is a surprisingly gripping mixture of personal history and psychological research. Perhaps the most intriguing web resource on the joys of solitude, meanwhile, is hermitary.com, a collection of writings and links on eremitism, or life as a hermit: deeply refreshing reading, even if you have no imminent plans to relocate to a cave.

3
HOW TO WIN FRIENDS AND
INFLUENCE PEOPLE: SOCIAL LIFE

If only because of its longevity and popularity, **Dale Carnegie's original book**, *How to Win Friends and Influence People* (Vermilion) repays reading; many smart and non-gullible people claim they've found much of value in it, even if I didn't. On the 'fundamental attribution error' – **how we blame other people's personalities for their behaviour** while finding situational excuses for our own – see Eliezer Yudkowsky's posting at overcomingbias.com/2007/06/correspondence.html, as well as a charming personal account of the problem by the Harvard psychologist Dan Gilbert entitled 'Speeding with Ned', in PDF form at wjh.harvard edu/~dtg/SpeedingwithNed.pdf. Andrea Donderi's original posting on **askers and guessers** is at ask.metafilter.com/ 55153/whats-the-middle-ground-between-fu-and-welcome# 830421. (A columnist for *The New Republic* makes his feelings on this subject very clear at tnr.com/blog/jonathan-chait/ ask-dont-guess.) The *Psychology Today* blog 'The Science of Small Talk', at psychologytoday.com/blog/science-small-talk, collects research on many other seemingly minor, but in fact ridiculously stress-inducing, aspects of day-to-day social interaction.

Russell Davies's blog post on **how to be interesting** is at russelldavies.typepad.com/planning/2006/11/how_to_be_ inter.html, while Mark Edmundson's essay on the curse of bores, especially in academia, is at theamericanscholar.org/ enough-already. (Good conversation, he argues, should resemble a tennis game, whereas 'to the bore a conversation is like a tennis game where he gathers up all the balls from the court and begins hitting them at you as hard and fast as possible'.) The most accessible collection of research on **the science of romantic compatibility**, meanwhile, is Tara Parker-Pope's book *For Better (For Worse): The Science of a Good Marriage* (Vermilion); Po Bronson's *Why Do I Love These People* (Vintage) is a moving interview-based book on marriage, children, and family life in general. The strange irrationalities of sexual attraction and romantic relationships is also one of the favourite topics of the indefatigable psychology-blogger Eric Barker, at bakadesuyo.com or on Twitter as @bakadesuyo.

The so-called **Ben Franklin effect** is far from Franklin's only contribution to the topics of psychology, personal development and productivity: you can't help feeling he'd have been entirely at home browsing a modern-day bookstore's 'popular psychology' section. A good blog post on Franklin and happiness, with a link to the full text of his *Autobiography*, is at 43folders.com/2005/09/01/ben-franklin-keeper-of-his-own-permanent-record.

Stan James's posting on **how quasi-friends can make you feel bad**, because you only hear the highlights of their lives, is called 'Facebook Acquaintances the New TV Stars', and is at wanderingstan.com/2010-07-22/facebook-acquaintances-the-new-tv-stars. A post by Ben Casnocha at ben.casnocha.com/2006/07/personal_blogs_.html makes a similar point, but from a more positive angle: if you've already decided that you're going to blog about, or otherwise broadcast, an experience in advance, does that make you more likely consciously to make it an enjoyable one?

4
HOW TO RULE THE OFFICE: WORK LIFE

The management philosophy of Craiglists's Jim Buckmaster – including his absolutist rejection of the whole idea of **meetings** – is summarised in a profile by the *Financial Times* journalist Lucy Kellaway, reprinted on Craigslist's website at sfbay.craigslist.org/about/press/ft.lucy. (Another of his mottoes: Put speed over perfection. 'Get something out there. Do it, even if it isn't perfect.') Cali Ressler and Jody Thompson's book *Why Work Sucks and How to Fix It* (Portfolio) pushes the idea further, and will provide good ammunition if you're planning to negotiate a work-from-home agreement with your employer. If you manage other people, though, its vision of a 'results-only work environment' may prove challenging reading: would you be willing to sacrifice *every* measure of your workers' performance – their presence at meetings, their time of arrival at their desk in the morning – if it meant they'd do their jobs better? For a similarly radical rethinking of how work life is structured, see *The Way We're Working Isn't Working* (Simon & Schuster) by Tony Schwartz, Jean Gomes and Catherine McCarthy, and its accompanying website theenergyproject.com.

One of the studies on **interruptions at work** that ignited the current new interest in the topic was carried out by researchers at Microsoft; it's a fairly easy read and is downloadable in PDF form at research.microsoft.com/en-us/um/people/horvitz/taskdiary.pdf. Jason Fried, a founder of the innovative software company 37 Signals, offers his thoughts on how the modern workplace is 'optimised for interruptions' – and what to do about it – in a video interview at bigthink.com/ideas/18522.

It's frustratingly hard to track down copies of C. Northcote Parkinson's original book *Parkinson's Law or The Pursuit of Progress* (Penguin), which contains his law of triviality – also known as **the 'colour of the bike shed' effect** – as well as the better-known observation about work expanding to fill the time available, and many others. But it's worth trying to find: Parkinson's pithy analyses of the irrationalities of organisational life remain as pertinent today as ever. Another good insight: 'The man who is denied the opportunity of taking decisions of importance begins to regard as important the decisions he is allowed to take.'

What Do I Do When I Want to Do Everything? (Rodale, also published as *Refuse to Choose*), Barbara Sher's monumentally reassuring book on why it's OK to be **a generalist rather than a specialist**, is one of several admirably sane works she's written on the topic of careers. Another is *I Could Do Anything If I Only Knew What It Was* (Bantam), while her website, barbarasher.com, includes large amounts of free material and a lively discussion forum.

Unlike *Parkinson's Law*, Laurence J. Peter and Raymond
Hull's *The Peter Principle* – which sets out Peter's satirical-yet-
accurate theories on **incompetence** in business life – is
easily available, published in editions by HarperBusiness and
Souvenir Press. The Dunning–Kruger effect, whereby the
most incompetent people most over-rate their competence
because they're too useless to realise how useless they are,
has enjoyed a resurgence in popularity recently. One great
analysis, including an interview with David Dunning, is in a
post by the filmmaker Errol Morris, at opinionator.blogs.
nytimes.com/2010/06/20/the-anosognosics-dilemma-1. It
includes the tale of the bank robber who was mystified to be
caught via security camera footage, because he'd smeared
lemon juice on his face. And everyone knows lemon juice
makes you invisible to security cameras . . . right? If he was
too stupid to be a bank robber, Morris writes, 'perhaps he
was also too stupid to know that he was too stupid to be a
bank robber'.

5
HOW TO GET MORE DONE: PRODUCTIVITY

Over the last few decades, so many books on productivity
have been published that there's a major risk of spending so
much time exploring them that you never get around to doing
anything. The huge growth of productivity blogs and
'lifehacking' websites over the last few years has rendered this
problem many times worse. If you consider yourself addicted
to such books, please read Merlin Mann's tirade against
'productivity tips', at 43folders.com/2008/12/03/real-advice-
hurts, then go and do some work.

If you're still here, perhaps because you're beset by

procrastination, a crucial book to read is *The Now Habit* (Wiley) by Neil Fiore. His methods for short-circuiting the problem focus on building a schedule that includes plenty of high-quality leisure time. Our efforts to force ourselves to do more and more work, he argues, are counterproductive, because we rebel against them; far better to guarantee ourselves plenty of time off, then fit work into the small, unintimidating slots that remain. (Fiore's advice is aimed at students, and harder to implement if you're employed, but the principle is still worth grasping.) John Perry's sardonic essay 'Structured Procrastination', at structuredprocrastination.com, explains how to use procrastination to your advantage, echoing Robert Benchley's venerable advice in 'How to Get Things Done', online at hackvan.com/etext/how-to-get-things-done-despite-procrastination.txt. 'Anyone can do any amount of work,' Benchley points out, 'provided it isn't the work he is supposed to be doing at that moment.'

Email management is only one of many topics addressed in David Allen's *Getting Things Done* (Piatkus), a work that has become the bible of a new generation of productivity obsessives. The full 'GTD' productivity system can get complicated, but its underlying philosophy can be adopted more simply. Much stress, Allen theorises, results from our brains being poor storage mechanisms for remembering everything on our plates, and from our failing to clarify exactly what we need to do next. By storing lists of 'next actions' in a single 'trusted system', outside our heads, he says, it's possible to achieve a 'mind like water'. Harvard Business School also offers detailed advice on email management at hbswk.hbs.edu/archive/4438.html. Implementing Allen's GTD system is one way to **overhaul your to-do list**, but there are many others, several of them on the website of Mark Forster at markforster.net. His ultra-simple Autofocus system – utilising the concept of the 'closed list' – is at markforster.net/blog/ 2009/1/6/autofocus-system-instructions.html.

The notion that creativity thrives on constraint is one of several aspects of **how to have ideas** addressed in Scott Berkun's book *The Myths of Innovation* (O'Reilly Media), and in 'Design Under Constraint: How Limits Boost Creativity', a showcase of inventions in *Wired* magazine at wired.com/ culture/design/magazine/17-03/dp_intro. And if you're intent on **becoming an early riser**, Steve Pavlina's perhaps overly detailed guide is in two parts at stevepavlina.com/ blog/2005/05/how-to-become-an-early-riser and stevepavlina. com/blog/2005/05/how-to-become-an-early-riser-part-ii. Leo Babauta, who says he gets up at 4.30 a.m. – I've no reason to disbelieve him – offers his thoughts on the matter at zenhabits.net/10-benefits-of-rising-early-and-how-to-do-it. To compare your habits with history's greatest artists and writers, see the addictive blog Daily Routines at dailyroutines. typepad.com. Structure your day, down to the minute, exactly like that of Saul Bellow or Simone de Beauvoir, and who knows what greatness might result? Or not.

6
HOW TO USE YOUR BRAIN: MENTAL LIFE

The cognitive biases and other mental phenomena discussed throughout this chapter are covered by two excellent UK-based blogs, Mind Hacks (mindhacks.com) and PsyBlog (spring.org.uk), as well as in Dan Ariely's two books *Predictably Irrational* and *The Upside of Irrationality* (both published by HarperCollins).

There are countless books and websites promising to tell you **how to remember things**, but one of the most interesting is Piotr Wozniak's SuperMemo (supermemo.com), which promotes a method of memorisation that exploits the principle of 'spaced repetition'. According to this notion, the best time to embed something deeply in your brain is when you're on the verge of forgetting it; SuperMemo is designed to present you with the material you're trying to remember at exactly that optimum point. It's available as a computer program, but there are instructions for how to do it with paper and pen, too. It's particularly useful for language learners.

A good primer on **the psychology of money** is entitled, appropriately enough *The Psychology of Money* (Routledge), by Adrian Furnham and Michael Argyle, while there's a detailed summary of the research into our irrational attitudes to cash, along with many links to studies, at spring.org.uk/2008/03/whistlestop-tour-of-research-on.php. The American economist Tyler Cowen's book *Discover Your Inner Economist* (Plume) examines many money-related conundrums – why, for example, your children might be *less* likely to do chores around the house if you pay them – while also applying economic thinking to non-financial daily life. For much more of that latter approach, see Tim Harford's extremely readable books *The Undercover Economist* and *Dear Undercover Economist* (both published by Abacus).

Paul Thagard's definitive paper on **whether to trust your brain or your gut** is available online at cogsci.uwaterloo.ca/Articles/Pages/how-to-decide.html, and Malcolm Gladwell's *Blink* (Penguin) is the definitive popular study of both the promise and the dangers of intuitive decision-making. Dan Ariely gives a short talk at the TED conference on related issues – and on the alarming question of whether we can truly be said to be in charge of our own decisions at all – at ted.com/talks/dan_ariely_asks_are_we_in_control_of_our_own_decisions.html.

Marti Laney's book *The Introvert Advantage* (Workman) has been joined more recently by Laurie Helgoe's *Introvert Power* (Sourcebooks) in the field of reassuring, research-based reads on the **upsides of being an introvert**; many introverts have also sought, and usually received, wise advice from the contributors to the website Ask Metafilter at ask.metafilter.com/tags/introvert. Sophia Dembling runs an introvert-specific blog with the arguably highly appropriate title *The Introvert's Corner* at psychologytoday.com/blog/the-introverts-corner.

Robert Cialdini's *Influence* (Harper Business) is an almost too fascinating manual on the dark arts of **persuasion**, rounding up a huge amount of research on everything from the Jonestown Massacre to the secret persuasion techniques of car salesmen, with plenty of Machiavellian humour. It feels as if it ought to come with a warning not to use its powers for evil.

7
HOW TO KEEP FUNCTIONING:
EVERYDAY LIFE

The always thorny challenge of **how to break bad habits** – and how to inculcate new and better ones – is one of the favourite topics of personal development bloggers and speakers everywhere, but the quality of their advice varies wildly; one of the best online resources is My Bad Habits, the blog of the Canadian academic Ian Newby-Clark (my-bad-habits.blogspot.com). Although it may be a myth that it takes 28 days to develop a new habit, there's also much to be said for the '30-day trial technique', recommended by Steve Pavlina at stevepavlina.com/blog/2005/04/30-days-to-success. Committing to a new behaviour for 30 days may be overkill for some habits and insufficient for others, but it works well as a motivator: it represents a sizeable chunk of time – enough to notice a real difference, if your plan is, say, to exercise more or to get enough sleep – yet remains essentially unintimidating. Deciding to stop eating junk food for the rest of your life may be a hard idea to get your head around. Deciding to do it for 30 days, knowing you'll be free to revert to your old ways after that if you choose, is much more manageable.

The **new frugality movement** is centred on several popular blogs, including getrichslowly.org, thesimpledollar.com, and frugal.families.com, but owes much of its modern-day popularity to the 1992 book *Your Money or Your Life* (Penguin), by Joe Dominguez and Vicki Robin (not to be confused with other books of the same title). Rather than urging strict budgeting and self-denial, Dominguez and Robin encourage you to see your spending as an expenditure of 'life energy' – the time and effort involved in working to amass money in the first place – and therefore to realise that spending less, and quite possibly working less, may be the path to a more enjoyable and more leisure-filled life.

The always-connected, information-overloaded society that prompts some people to recommend **going on a news diet** is usually seen as a modern phenomenon. But as William Powers shows in his entertaining book *Hamlet's BlackBerry* (Harper), the idea that we might need to manage, consciously, the daily onrush of information is one that has concerned philosophers and scholars for centuries. Powers offers, in the words of his book's subtitle, 'a practical philosophy for building a good life in the digital age'.

E.M. Cioran's unconventional views on **insomnia** are discussed at length in Gordon Marino's essay 'Counting the "Blessings" of Insomnia', at opinionator.blogs.nytimes.com/2010/03/29/counting-the-blessings-of-insomnia. For more practical advice, it's worth tracking down Lawrence Epstein's *The Harvard Medical School Guide to a Good Night's Sleep* (McGraw-Hill), while Sara Mednick's book *Take a Nap! Change Your Life* (Workman) makes the case for Winston Churchill-style midday sleep catchups. It comes with a moveable 'nap wheel' on the cover, designed to help you calculate when best to grab a few minutes' rest on the sofa, or under your desk, for maximum effectiveness.

Doug Dyment's website onebag.com remains the (slightly obsessive) ultimate source on **travelling light**, while the equally irrepressible Tim Ferriss has a video tutorial entitled 'How to Travel the World With 10lbs or Less' at fourhourworkweek.com/blog/2007/07/11. Travellers share their tips at http://www.ricksteves.com/graffiti/graffiti82.html, while a US-published book, Judith Gilford's *The Packing Book: Secrets of the Carry-On Traveler* (Ten Speed) offers many more pieces of advice. If you buy it, though, be sure to digest its wisdom and then leave it at home, or you'll make your bag heavier, not lighter.

8
FOLLOW ME: GURUS, GOD-MEN AND OTHER QUESTIONABLE CHARACTERS

Perhaps unsurprisingly for a controversial system that claims to offer a 'revolutionary' approach to almost every aspect of human interaction, the world of **neuro-linguistic programming** has splintered into a feuding cacophony of rival organisations and experts, but there are some saner voices to be heard amid the noise. A widely respected introductory book is *NLP: The New Technology of Achievement* (Nicholas Brealey), edited by Steve Andreas and Charles Faulkner, while there's plenty of level-headed material on the website of NLP School Europe at nlpschooleurope.com. George Miller's celebrated (and funny) paper on the strange ubiquity of **the number seven**, entitled 'The magical number seven, plus or minus two: some limits on our capacity for processing information' is available online at psychclassics.yorku.ca/Miller.

Alan Watts's autobiography *In My Own Way* (New World Library), though hardly a neutral source on Watts's own life, is excellent on the subject of **gurus and fraudsters**, and the perhaps unavoidably blurred line between the two. Anthony Storr's *Feet of Clay: A Study of Gurus* (HarperCollins) identifies intriguing commonalities among history's high-profile gurus, from Gurdjieff, Freud and Jung to the likes of the messianic cult leader David Koresh. For a significantly more easygoing account of life among the gurus, see Mick Brown's *The Spiritual Tourist* (Bloomsbury).

9
ROADS LESS TRAVELLED: SOME UNLIKELY PATHS TO HAPPINESS

The surprisingly deep insight contained in the old cliché **'if it ain't broke, don't fix it'** is explored at length in Barry Magid's book *Ending the Pursuit of Happiness: A Zen Guide* (Wisdom); it's aimed primarily at Buddhist meditation students, but don't let that put you off. There's an interview with Magid at sweepingzen.com/2009/12/25/barry-magid-interview.

The idea that it's more beneficial to **focus on process rather than outcome** is one of the key messages of John Eliot's book *Overachievement* (Portfolio), which applies the lessons of sports science to performance in all areas of life. It's also an implicit message throughout *The Power of Full*

Engagement (Free Press), by Jim Loehr and Tony Schwartz, which seeks to replace the notion of 'time management' with 'energy management'. The Japanese industrial strategy of *kaizen* – which focuses on continual improvements in process rather than an unrelenting fixation on goals and outcomes – is relevant here, too; a book that applies its principles beyond management to daily life and personal psychology is Robert Maurer's *One Small Step Can Change Your Life: The Kaizen Way* (Workman).

Robert Anton Wilson's characteristically wild-eyed but still highly thought-provoking essay on **E-prime, or writing without using the verb 'to be'**, from his book *Quantum Psychology* (New Falcon), is available at rawilson.com/quantum.html. And on the topic of **embracing imperfection**, see the essay 'The Elegance of Imperfection', by David Sherwin, at alistapart.com/articles/the-elegance-of-imperfection – it's explicitly about designing websites, but it's also really about designing life. The aesthetic of *wabi-sabi*, in particular, is explored in '*Wabi-Sabi*: The Art of Imperfection', at utne.com/2001-09-01/Wabi-Sabi.aspx. '*Wabi-sabi* is the art of finding beauty in imperfection and profundity in earthiness,' the author writes. '[It] reminds us that we are all transient beings on this planet – that our bodies, as well as the material world around us, are in the process of returning to dust.'

NOTES

1   Research on the fixed aspects of personality is discussed in Sonja Lyubomirsky, *The How of Happiness* (New York: Penguin Press, 2007), chapter one.

2   See Carol Dweck, *Mindset: The New Psychology of Success* (New York: Ballantine Books, 2007).

3   David Schkade and Daniel Kahneman, 'Does living in California make people happy? A focusing illusion in judgments of life satisfaction', *Psychological Science* 9 (1998): 340–346.

4   The research on self-deception and denial is voluminous. One recent example is Nina Mazar et al, 'The dishonesty of honest people: a theory of self-concept maintenance', *Journal of Marketing Research* 45 (2008): 633–644.

5   Jennifer Gregg et al, 'Improving diabetes self-management through acceptance, mindfulness, and values: a randomized controlled trial', *Journal of Consulting and Clinical Psychology* 75 (2007): 336–343.

6   Lawrence Tabak, 'If your goal is success, don't consult these gurus', *Fast Company* (December 1996).

7   Kim Baskerville et al, 'Reactions to random acts of kindness', *Social Science Journal* 37 (2000): 293–298.

8   Much of the research on the benefits of novel experience is collected in Todd Kashdan, *Curious? Discover the Missing Ingredient to a Fulfilling Life* (New York: William Morrow, 2009).

9   Mark Easton, 'Britain's happiness in decline', BBC News website, May 2, 2006, accessible at news.bbc.co.uk/2/hi/programmes/happiness_formula/4771908.stm.

10   For a summary of Michael McCullough and Robert Emmons's gratitude research, with references to individual journal articles, see psychology.ucdavis.edu/labs/emmons/ or Robert Emmons, *Thanks! How the New Science of Gratitude Can Make You Happier* (New York: Houghton Mifflin, 2007). See also note 1.

11 Martin Seligman et al, 'Positive psychology progress: empirical validation of interventions', *American Psychologist* 60 (2005): 410–421.

12 See, for example, Robert Emmons and Michael McCullough, 'Counting blessings versus burdens: an experimental investigation of gratitude and subjective well-being in daily life', *Journal of Personality and Social Psychology* 84 (2003): 377–389.

13 Andrea diMartini et al, 'Post-traumatic stress disorder caused by hallucinations and delusions experienced in delirium', *Psychosomatics* 48 (2007): 436–439.

14 Jorge Moll et al, 'Human fronto-mesolimbic networks guide decisions about charitable donation', *Proceedings of the National Academy of Sciences* 103 (2006): 15623–15628.

15 Footage of Dawkins taking questions from creationist students, including a discussion of altruism, is at video.google.com/videoplay?docid=-8033327978006186584#.

16 Sandy Wolfson and Pamela Briggs, 'Locked into gambling: anticipatory regret as a motivator for playing the National Lottery', *Journal of Gambling Studies* 18 (2002): 1–17.

17 Roese's research is discussed in Neal Roese, *If Only* (New York: Broadway, 2005). For further evidence that inaction is regretted more than action, see Marcel Zeelenberg et al, 'The inaction effect in the psychology of regret', *Journal of Personality and Social Psychology* 82 (2002): 314–327. Several earlier studies reached an opposite conclusion, but Zeelenberg et al suggest this may be because they studied isolated, one-off decisions in artificial experimental settings.

18 Neal Roese and Amy Summerville, 'What we regret most . . . and why', *Personality and Social Psychology Bulletin* 31 (2005): 1273–1285.

19 Robert Provine's research on laugh-trigger phrases, the link between laughter and humour, and the role of laughter in personal advertisements is detailed in his book *Laughter: A Scientific Investigation* (New York: Viking, 2000).

20 James Pennebaker and Sandra Beall, 'Confronting a traumatic event: towards an understanding of inhibition and disease', *Journal of Abnormal Psychology* 95 (1986): 274–281.

21 John Weinman et al, 'Enhanced wound healing after an emotional disclosure intervention', *British Journal of Health Psychology* 13 (2008): 95–102.

22 If you're part of a married couple, anyway. The paper in question is Jean Twenge et al, 'Parenthood and marital satisfaction: a meta-analytic review', *Journal of Marriage and Family* 65 (2003): 574–583.

23 Nattavudh Powdthavee, 'Think having children will make you happy?', *The Psychologist* 22 (2009): 308–310.

24 Philip Brickman et al, 'Lottery winners and accident victims: is happiness relative?', *Journal of Personality and Social Psychology* 37 (1978): 917–927.

25 Daniel Simons and Daniel Levin, 'Failure to detect changes to people during a real-world interaction', *Psychonomic Bulletin and Review* 5 (1998): 644–649.

26 Scott Taylor, 'An exploration of wilderness effects: a phenomenological inquiry', online at www.c-zone.net/taylors.

27 These findings are from Robert Wuthnow, 'Peak experiences: some empirical tests', *Journal of Humanistic Psychology* 18 (1978): 59–75 and Andrew Greeley, *Ecstasy: A Way of Knowing* (New York: Prentice Hall, 1974): 141.

28 See Martin Seligman, *Helplessness* (San Francisco: Freeman, 1975).

29 For example, Brad Bushman, 'Does venting anger feed or extinguish the flame? Catharsis, rumination, distraction, anger, and aggressive responding', *Personality and Social Psychology Bulletin* 28 (2002): 724–731.

30 R.H. Hornberger, 'The differential reduction of aggressive responses as a function of interpolated activities', *American Psychologist*, 14 (1959): 354.

31 Lisa Starr and Joanne Davila, 'Clarifying co-rumination: associations with internalizing symptoms and romantic involvement among adolescent girls', *Journal of Adolescence* 32 (2009): 19–37.

32 Richard Wiseman summarised his findings, based on surveys conducted at a science festival, in 'The truth about lying and laughing', *The Guardian*, 21 April 2007, at

www.guardian.co.uk/science/2007/apr/21/weekendmagazine.

33 F. Strack et al, 'Inhibiting and facilitating conditions of the human smile: a nonobtrusive test of the facial feedback hypothesis', *Journal of Personality and Social Psychology* 54 (1988): 768–777.

34 The story of Hans Selye, stress and strain is summarised at the website of the American Institute of Stress, www.stress.org/hans.htm.

35 Bert Brown, 'Face-saving following experimentally induced embarrassment', *Journal of Experimental Social Psychology* 6 (1970): 255–271.

36 Christine Harris, 'Embarrassment: a form of social pain', *American Scientist* 94 (2006) 524–533.

37 Ibid.

38 Much of the research on embarrassment involved Rowland Miller, and is discussed in his book *Embarrassment: Poise and Peril in Everyday Life* (New York: Guilford Press, 1996).

39 Barbara Fredrickson and Marcial Losada, 'Positive affect and the complex dynamics of human flourishing', *American Psychologist*, 60 (2005): 678–686; and Barbara Fredrickson, *Positivity: Groundbreaking Research Reveals How to Embrace the Hidden Strength of Positive Emotions, Overcome Negativity, and Thrive* (New York: Crown, 2009).

40 J.P. Forgas and S. Moylan, 'After the movies: the effects of transient mood states on social judgments', *Personality and Social Psychology Bulletin* 13 (1987): 478–489.

41 These findings are discussed throughout John Cacioppo, *Loneliness: Human Nature and the Need for Social Connection* (New York: W.W. Norton, 2008).

42 C.-B. Zhong and G.L. Leonardelli, 'Cold and lonely: does social exclusion literally feel cold?', *Psychological Science* 19 (2008): 838–842.

43 Cacioppo, op. cit. (See note 41).

44 E.E. Jones and V.A. Harris, 'The attribution of attitudes', *Journal of Experimental Social Psychology* 3 (1967): 1–24.

45 J.G. Miller, 'Culture and the development of everyday social

explanation', *Journal of Personality and Social Psychology* 46 (1984): 961–978.

46 Philip Zimbardo, 'A situationist perspective on the psychology of evil: understanding how good people are transformed into perpetrators', in Arthur Miller, ed, *The Social Psychology of Good and Evil: Understanding Our Capacity for Kindness and Cruelty* (New York: Guilford, 2005).

47 Scott Feld, 'Why your friends have more friends than you do', *American Journal of Sociology* 96 (1991): 1464–77.

48 Satoshi Kanazawa, 'Why your friends have more friends than you do', *Psychology Today*, November 1, 2009, online at www.psychologytoday.com/blog/the-scientific-fundamentalist/200911/why-your-friends-have-more-friends-you-do.

49 Andrea Donderi's posting, under the username 'tangerine', is online at ask.metafilter.com/55153/whats-the-middle-ground-between-fu-and-welcome#830421.

50 See, for example, research by Stephen Emlen and Peter Buston, summarised in Catherine Zandonella, 'Opposites do not attract in mating game', *New Scientist* 30 (June 2003), at www.newscientist.com/article/dn3887-opposites-do-not-attract-in-mating-game.html.

51 Robert Epstein, 'How science can help you fall in love', *Scientific American Mind* Jan–Feb 2010: 26–33.

52 Ibid.

53 One real-life example is Thomas Walker and Eleanor Main, 'Choice shifts in political decisionmaking: federal judges and civil liberties cases', *Journal of Applied Social Psychology* 3 (2006): 39–48.

54 For example, Miron Zuckerman et al, 'The egocentric bias: seeing oneself as cause and target of others' behaviour', *Journal of Personality* 51 (2006): 621–630.

55 Thomas Gilovich et al, 'The spotlight effect in social judgment: an egocentric bias in estimates of the salience of one's own actions and appearance', *Journal of Personality and Social Psychology* 78 (2000): 211–222.

56 Jon Jecker and David Landy, 'Liking a person as a function of doing him a favour', *Human Relations* 22 (1969): 371–378.

57 One such recent study is S. Goel et al, 'Real and perceived attitude homophily in social networks', a report for Yahoo! Research (2010), available online at www.cam.cornell.edu/~sharad/papers/friendsense.pdf.

58 William Swann and Michael Gill, 'Confidence and accuracy in person perception: do we know what we think we know about our relationship partners?', *Journal of Personality and Social Psychology* 73 (1997): 747–757.

59 Solomon Asch, 'Opinions and social pressure', *Scientific American* 193 (1955): 31–35.

60 See for example Mark Granovetter, 'The strength of weak ties: a network theory revisited', *Sociological Theory* 1 (1983): 201–233.

61 Robert Nelson and Peter Economy, *Better Business Meetings* (Burr Ridge, Illinois: Irwin Professional Publishing): 5.

62 Zoltán Dornyeï, *The Psychology of the Language Learner* (Mahwah, New Jersey: Laurence Erlbaum Associates, 2005): 158.

63 Steven Rogelberg et al, '"Not another meeting!": are meeting time demands related to employee wellbeing?' *Journal of Applied Psychology* 1 (2006): 86–96.

64 Discussed in Mary Czerwinski et al, 'A diary study of task switching and interruptions', *Proceedings of the SIGCHI Conference on Human Factors in Computing Systems* (2004): 175–182.

65 Cameron Anderson and Gavin Kilduff, 'Why do dominant personalities attain influence in face-to-face groups? The competence-signaling effects of trait dominance', *Journal of Personality and Social Psychology* 96 (2009): 491–503.

66 K. Weaver et al, 'Inferring the popularity of an opinion from its familiarity: a repetitive voice can sound like a chorus', *Journal of Personality and Social Psychology* 92 (2007): 821–833.

67 This research is collected in Dalton Conley, *Elsewhere, USA: How We Got from the Company Man, Family Dinners, and the Affluent Society to the Home Office, BlackBerry Moms, and Economic Anxiety* (New York: Pantheon, 2009).

68 Winifred Gallagher, *Rapt: Attention and the Focused Life* (New York: Penguin Press, 2009): 109, referring to research by Mihaly Csikszentmihalyi.

69 Justin Kruger and David Dunning, 'Unskilled and unaware of it: how difficulties of recognizing one's own incompetence lead to inflated self-assessments', *Journal of Personality and Social Psychology* 77 (1999): 1121–1134.

70 In Marcus Buckingham and Donald Clifton, *Now, Discover Your Strengths* (New York: Simon and Schuster, 2001).

71 J. Harriott and J.R. Ferrari, 'Prevalence of procrastination among samples of adults', *Psychological Reports* 78 (1996): 611–616.

72 The definitive resource on the Hawthorne experiments is on Harvard Business School's website at www.library.hbs.edu/hc/hawthorne/.

73 For example, see 'Survey finds workers average only three productive days per week,' Microsoft news release, 15 March 2005, at www.microsoft.com/presspass/press/2005/mar05/03-15threeproductivedayspr.mspx.

74 R. Buehler et al, 'Exploring the 'planning fallacy': why people underestimate their task completion times', *Journal of Personality and Social Psychology* 67 (1994): 366–381.

75 Most terrifyingly, see www.flickr.com/photos/hawkexpress/sets/72157594200490122/.

76 Mary Czerwinski, op cit. (See note 64.)

77 Warren St John and Alex Williams, 'The crow of the early bird', *New York Times*, 27 March 2005.

78 K. Dijkstra et al, 'Body posture facilitates retrieval of autobiographical memories', *Cognition* 102 (2007): 139–149.

79 For example, Christopher Boyce et al, 'Money and happiness: rank of income, not income, affects life satisfaction', *Psychological Science* 21 (2010): 471–475.

80 Daniel Kahneman et al, 'The endowment effect, loss aversion, and status quo bias', *Journal of Economic Perspectives* (1991): 193–206.

81 Amos Tversky and Daniel Kahneman, 'The framing of decisions and the psychology of choice', *Science* 211 (1981): 453–458.

82 Robert Lemlich's work on the experience of time passing is discussed in Jay Ingram, *The Velocity of Honey* (New York: Basic Books, 2006):191–193.

258   OLIVER BURKEMAN

83 Petter Johansson et al, 'Failure to detect mismatches between intention and outcome in a simple decision task', *Science* 310 (2005): 116–119.

84 Richard Nisbett and Timothy Wilson, 'Telling more than we can know: verbal reports on mental processes', *Psychological Review* 84 (1977): 231–259.

85 Ap Dijksterhuis, 'On making the right choice: the deliberation-without-attention effect', *Science* 311(2006): 1005–1007.

86 Hyunjin Song and Norbert Schwarz, 'If it's hard to read, it's hard to do: processing fluency affects effort prediction and motivation', *Psychological Science* 19 (2008): 986–988.

87 Mark Rubin et al, 'A processing fluency explanation of bias against migrants', *Journal of Experimental Social Psychology* 46 (2010): 21–28.

88 Adam Alter and Daniel Oppenheimer, 'Predicting short-term stock fluctuations by using processing fluency', *Proceedings of the National Academy of Sciences* 103 (2006): 9369–9372.

89 Daniel Wegner, 'How to think, say or do precisely the worst thing for any occasion', *Science* 325 (2009): 48–50.

90 J. L. Freedman and S. C. Fraser, 'Compliance without pressure: the foot-in-the-door technique', *Journal of Personality and Social Psychology* 4 (1966): 196–202.

91 Robert Knox and James Inkster, 'Postdecision dissonance at post time', *Journal of Personality and Social Psychology* 8 (1968): 319–323.

92 Dan Ariely and Michael Norton, 'Conceptual consumption', *Annual Review of Psychology* 60 (2009): 475–499.

93 B.F. Skinner, '"Superstition" in the pigeon', *Journal of Experimental Psychology* 38 (1948): 168–172.

94 Matthew Gailliot et al, 'Self-control relies on glucose as a limited energy source: willpower is more than a metaphor', *Journal of Personality and Social Psychology* 92 (2007): 325–336.

95 Ibid.

96 Ran Kivetz and Anat Keinan, 'Repenting hyperopia: an analysis of self-control regrets', *Journal of Consumer Research* 33 (2006): 273–282.

97 Ran Kivetz and Itamar Simonson, 'Self-control for the righteous:

towards a theory of precommitment to indulgence', *Journal of Consumer Research* 29 (2002): 119–217.

98   Brooks Gump and Karen Matthews, 'Do background stressors influence reactivity to and recovery from acute stressors?', *Journal of Applied Social Psychology* 29 (2006): 469–494.

99   Andrew Baum, Jerome Singer and Carlene Baum, 'Stress and the environment', in Gary W. Evans, ed, *Environmental Stress* (Cambridge: Cambridge University Press, 1983).

100 'The case for smarter commuting', Citrix Online, November 2009, available online at www.workshifting.com/Commute SmartWhitepaper.pdf.

101 For example, Alois Stutzer, 'Commuting and happiness', presentation to the AGS Annual Meeting 2009, available online at www.cces.ethz.ch/agsam2009/panels/AGSAM2009_panel_mobility_Stutzer.pdf.

102 Alois Stutzer and Bruno Frey, 'Stress that doesn't pay: the commuting paradox', *Scandinavian Journal of Economics* 110 (2008): 339–366.

103 Alpaslan Akay and Peter Martinsson, 'Sundays are blue: aren't they? The day-of-the-week effect on subjective well-being and socio-economic Status', *IZA Discussion Paper* 4563 (2009).

104 Phillippa Lally et al, 'How are habits formed: modelling habit formation in the real world', *European Journal of Social Psychology*, published online July 2009. See www3.interscience.wiley.com/journal/122513384/abstract.

105 Ellen Furlong and John Opfner, 'Cognitive constraints on how economic rewards affect cooperation', *Psychological Science* 20 (2009): 11–16.

106 Stanley Milgram et al, 'Response to intrusion into waiting lines', *Journal of Personality and Social Psychology* 51 (1986): 683–689.

107 David Maister, 'The psychology of waiting lines', in J.A. Czepiel et al, eds, *The Service Encounter: Managing Employee–Customer Interaction in Service Businesses* (Lexington, Massachusetts: Lexington Books, 1985).

108 Francesco Cappuccio et al, 'Sleep duration and all-cause mortality: a systematic review and meta-analysis of prospective studies', *Sleep* 33 (2010): 585–592.

109 P.M. Todd, 'Searching for the next best mate', in R. Conte et al, eds, *Lecture Notes in Economics and Mathematical Systems* (Berlin: Springer-Verlag, 1997): 419–436.

110 Arline Bronzaft, 'Beware: noise is hazardous to our children's development', *Hearing Rehabilitation Quarterly* 22 (1997) and M.M. Haines et al, 'Multilevel modelling of aircraft noise on performance tests in schools around Heathrow airport, London', *Journal of Epidemiology and Community Health* 56 (2002): 139–144.

111 Staffan Hygge et al, 'The Munich airport noise study: cognitive effects on children from before to after the changeover of airports', in *Noise Control – The Next 25 Years (Inter Noise 96 Conference)*, F.A. Hill and R. Lawrence eds, 5 (1996): 2189–2192, and Gary Evans et al, 'Chronic noise exposure and physiological response: a prospective study of children living under environmental stress', *Psychological Science* 9 (1998): 75–77.

112 Stefan Willich et al, 'Noise burden and the risk of myocardial infarction', *European Heart Journal* 27 (2006): 276–282.

113 Julie Norem and Nancy Cantor, 'Defensive pessimism: "harnessing" anxiety as motivation', *Journal of Personality and Social Psychology* 52 (1986): 1208–1217.

114 Discussed in Daniel Gilbert's TED talk, available online at http://www.ted.com/talks/dan_gilbert_asks_why_are_we_happy.html

115 See note 24.

116 Sonja Lyubomirsky, op. cit: 20. (See note 1.)

117 J.J. Skowronski et al, 'Spontaneous trait transference: communicators take on the qualities they describe in others', *Journal of Personality and Social Psychology* 74 (1998): 837–848.

118 George Miller, 'The magical number seven, plus or minus two: some limits on our capacity for processing information', *Psychological Review* 63 (1956): 81–97.

119 Bruce Wampold, *The Great Psychotherapy Debate: Models, Methods, and Findings* (London: Routledge, 2001).

120 Rob Stein, 'Revision to the bible of psychiatry, DSM, could introduce new mental disorders', *Washington Post*, 10 February 2010.

121 David Bourland, 'A linguistic note: writing in E-prime', *General Semantics Bulletin* 32 & 33 (1965).

122 'Shania Twain more beautiful than Angelina Jolie?', AFP report in the *Sydney Morning Herald*, 22 December 2009.

INDEX

ACKNOWLEDGEMENTS

The initial idea for the weekly column on which this book is based came from Merope Mills, the tirelessly inventive editor of the *Guardian*'s *Weekend* magazine and a great friend. For conveying it expertly to the page each week, I thank Emma Cook, Bob Granleese, Bill Mann, Andrea Chapman, Stephanie Fincham and Grainne Mooney. My gratitude journal (see page 31) should also include prominent entries for Claire Paterson; for Nick Davies and his brilliant colleagues at Canongate; for Esther Addley; for Ian Katz; and above all for my parents and sister. Thanks to Pascal Wyse for this book's title. I doubt I'd get much of anything done without the friendship of Emma Brockes, or of my friends from the north, of whom Daniel Weyman, Sally Weyman, Rachael Burnett and Robin Parmiter provided specific advice or assistance. Heather Chaplin was, and remains, remarkable.